ERIC HUDSON

I Love You, but I've Had Enough!

Managing a Relationship with a Partner Suffering from Borderline Personality Disorder

Contents

I

RECOGNIZING BPD

1

Introduction

This book is about romantic relationships that begin like a fantastic dream but later turn into a terrible nightmare. Did your love story start strongly, in a way that made you feel excited, hopeful and secure? Maybe you were even convinced that you had found your soulmate. Unfortunately, those happy moments turned out to be short lived, and your relationship spiraled into chaos and turmoil. Perhaps you are now experiencing frequent ups and downs, a pattern of fights and reconciliations with an underlying sense of uncertainty, instability and frustration. What went wrong?

Are you confused by your partner's frequent mood swings, their irrational fears of being left alone and their tendency to behave impulsively? These are the typical traits of a condition called Borderline Personality Disorder (BPD). What causes this condition?

How can you better recognize the signs of BPD? Above all, what can you do about your difficult and seemingly unmanageable relationship? Is it possible for the relationship to be nursed back to a healthy state? Or in the case of a break up, how can you learn to cope effectively? These questions and many others are answered in this book.

To illustrate all this, we begin with two real life examples of toxic relationships in which one partner suffers from Borderline Personality Disorder. These stories will serve as our starting point for the detailed analysis carried out in the book.

2

The Story of Jessica and Martin

Martin (33) started dating Jessica (26) shortly after moving to a new city to start a job as engineer for an energy company. Jessica is in college, studying for an MBA. The two met through a dating app and immediately established a strong connection from the very first night spent chatting online. After only a couple of dates, they decided to start a relationship. Martin saw Jessica as a special person, someone who was sensitive, intelligent, and shared many common interests with him. This gave him great hopes about the relationship.

Martin was a bit surprised to find out that Jessica lived a private and secluded life. According to her, the only people she talks to are her mom and her best friend Steven, with whom she admitted having had sex regularly for a year despite not feeling physically attracted to him. She never mentioned the rest of her family, and in particular avoided Martin's questions about her father. Perceiving her discomfort and afraid of conjuring up memories of painful episodes, he stopped asking about it.

The first difficulties in the relationship began after just a couple of weeks, when Jessica started behaving in a way that was totally incomprehensible to Martin. She started canceling plans at the last minute without any explanation. She would also disappear for days without warning, not answering texts or calls. When Martin tried to express his discomfort at such conduct, she accused him of being needy and obsessive. What he could not understand was the inconsistency of her attitude: one moment she would pull him close, only to push him away the next minute. How was it possible that after a perfect evening together she could just go missing for days, ignoring him completely? Was she playing with him? Such attitudes left him genuinely confused and unable to understand what was wrong with the relationship or how to fix it.

Despite the outgoing personality that she displayed in Martin's company, Jessica seemed to be remarkably insecure. Even after months of relationship, she still claimed to be not ready to meet his friends or family. She also appeared to be extremely jealous of his friends, and even of people from his past. Despite Martin's efforts to make her feel at ease, she never gave up her mistrustful attitude. Moreover, she seemed to be afraid of any form of commitment. She was always unwilling to promise to meet in a given day or even to talk on the phone at a certain time "What if I don't feel like it then?" Martin desperately wished to see her and therefore it was difficult for him to make other plans: he wanted to keep free for the rare moments in which she was willing to meet up. Once she got in touch unexpectedly after days of silence and when he answered the phone he was with his friends. She then took it personally, accusing him of hiding things from her, lying, and being unfaithful.

From the start of the relationship, the most worrying trait of Jessica's personality was her attraction to pain and hardship. She seemed to be purposefully looking for situations that are unpleasant and difficult. For instance, she once went three days without sleeping, claiming that "she likes feeling uncomfortable". Another time she slept on the roof on a chilly winter night. Once Martin asked her if she would like to have children eventually, and she said yes. Her motivation was that she wishes to "experience the pain of giving birth".

Martin, incapable to understand his partner and to manage the relationship in a way that would make him feel comfortable, started being overly affected by the situation. Unable to keep the level of concentration required for his job, he decided to quit, telling himself that probably it was not the career he really wanted. He started leading a more solitary life, alienating a lot of his friends and family members, and lying repeatedly to cover up his dysfunctional relationship and the fact that he was unemployed. Having progressively lost all his confidence and having become sort of resigned to his unhappiness, he eventually decided to seek professional help. After hearing his story, Martin's therapist told him that Jessica seems to exhibit a lot of the traits of a Borderline personality.

Jessica ended the relationship several times, saying that she was doing it for him, because she was "hurting him too much". After a couple of weeks, however, she would always come back, and they would try the relationship once again. Below, Martin tells his story during a therapy session, after what he believes to be the final breakup. Two days ago, when she called him on the phone and he was not at home, Jessica accused him of cheating and told him that she does not want to talk to him anymore. Martin seems convinced that this time he will not hear from her again.

I have spent the last twenty-four hours in bed, unable to move or do anything. It is not the first time; it has happened before, at each one of our breakups. She has already broken up with me four times in the last six months. Every time we started over, I have tried to stay positive and believe that things could be different. But nothing has really changed. If anything, things have gotten worse. What I cannot get my head around is the contrast between her words and her actions. She claims she loves me, and I can feel it when I look into her eyes. Yet she keeps behaving in a way that is completely unreasonable and leaves me hurt and confused. It is as if she can't control it.

The relationship with Jessica was my drug. It gave me peaks of ecstasy as well as long moments when I would feel miserable. I would have done anything to make it work. There was a sense of urgency and desperation in the way I went about managing the relationship. For example, I started lying a lot. I lied about this relationship to my friends and family, and I am truly ashamed about it. I feel that I have undermined the strong bond I had with them, especially with my mom and my brother. I did not tell them of the numerous breakups, always pretending that things were going well between me and Jessica. She has never met any of my friends or family members anyways, and therefore there was no risk that my deceptions would be uncovered.

One Sunday we had planned a day trip to a nearby town, but she canceled last minute for what I saw as no reason at all. I had told my family about the trip and ended up sending them pictures of the town that I found online pretending I had taken them myself. I did not want to have to explain her irrational behavior, I just couldn't. There was actually no sensible explanation I could offer. When I went to pick her up, she simply claimed to be afraid that she would miss me too much during the following week if we spent the entire day together. She said she loved me truly, but that I should not push her, that she needed her space, and she did not feel comfortable with how attached to each other we were getting. I could tell that she was genuinely distressed. But just the night before on the phone she had told me how excited she was for the trip, and at that time too she sounded sincere. How can a person change their mind so drastically and so quickly? This is inconceivable to me!

I sometimes lied to her as well. They were small lies, and you might consider them unnecessary, but I felt like I had no choice. Let me give you an example. One Saturday she did not answer my texts or calls all day. I had not seen her for two weeks, but she had hinted that we could probably meet that night. In the afternoon, after spending hours looking at my phone hoping for a message, I decided to take a long walk through the city by myself. I listened to an entire six-hour podcast, and only got back home quite late at night. I didn't tell her about it when she finally got in touch, saying instead that I had spent my evening at home reading and watching TV. It sounds silly that I felt the need to hide such an innocent thing as a stroll through the city. But I did not want her to know how I was feeling.

I have learned that when she behaves like this, going missing for many hours or even days, she expects some reaction from me, maybe an expression of rage, sadness, or frustration. Whatever it is, she will then focus on that reaction and start a fight. Therefore, I must pretend that everything is absolutely normal. Even when she reappears after days of silence, it is crucial that I make it look like I have gone on with my life as if nothing unusual has happened. Or there will be hell to pay. "When was the last time you took such a long walk? What was wrong? Why were you feeling bad? Because of me, surely. Because I can't do anything right, can I? Were you even alone in your walk, or were you seeing someone behind my back?" She will thus escalate the conversation, drawing sweeping conclusions from any word I utter. Whatever feeling I express, she will take it as an accusation, and I would instantly be blamed for it. But what should I have done differently? I took that walk only not to go crazy looking at my phone waiting for her verdict about seeing each other that night. Had she suggested meeting up, I would have just called a taxi and rushed home, and still I wouldn't have said a word about it. Does it make sense? Why is everything so difficult with her?

When I started going out with Jessica, I used to discuss the issues of the relationship with my close friends. But they would always tell me the same things that I didn't want to hear: "She is just messing with you. She must be seeing someone else. She is clearly not that much into you. Why else would she behave like that?" My friends are simply wrong here, and I stopped asking for their opinions. I can swear that Jessica is not putting up an act. I believe her when she says she loves me, and I am sure that she is not hurting me on purpose.

Once she told me that when she goes missing it is because she is trying to "suppress her feelings". She said she doesn't want to give in to her impulses and sometimes feels the need to fight them. I really can't relate to these arguments, but if I try to discuss with her, she immediately flares up, so I don't say anything and force myself to accept her views. I have the impression that she is just unable to manage her emotions in a healthy way and is often overwhelmed by them. Am I naive in accepting such explanations? Is it just wishful thinking on my part since I want to believe that her feelings for me are genuine? Is she faking it entirely, as my friends say?

I have many fantastic memories of my relationship with Jessica. She is amazing company when she is in a good mood, and we can then enjoy awesome date nights and great sex. She can be sweet, witty, and funny, and in these moments I want to believe that this is the real Jessica. She is also extremely sensitive and got me several meaningful gifts proving how well she knows me. She even wrote a poem for me! I love these intense moments together and I don't understand why it can't always be like that. But the happy times never last, and in the end, she always retreats in her shell. At that point, all my attempts at establishing some meaningful communication seem hopeless and are met with hostility. I just suffer immensely, and I don't know how to manage the situation.

I was addicted to her, and I suffered from withdrawal whenever she would suddenly grow silent and impenetrable. I could sense that in these moments she was not feeling good. I wanted to help her, but I didn't know how. I still don't know. I think she just can't accept that things might go well, and that she deserves to be happy. I have the impression that when something is functioning for her, she feels the need to sabotage it. How could I have stopped her self-destructive attitudes?

The fact that I would suddenly leave a person I was talking to or a friend with whom I was hanging out just to talk to her or see her says a lot about the level of my addiction, and how much I was affected by her mood swings. Once I was on an important online meeting with two colleagues when she unexpectedly called me on the phone. I had not heard from her for two days, so I abruptly interrupted the work call saying that I had a family emergency. She was my absolute priority, and I have many such examples. On these occasions I thought my behavior was justified, because I was acting for the good of the relationship. In retrospect those actions were just symptoms of my dependence, a sign that I was losing self-respect, and was enabling her to impose unchallenged her views about the relationship.

Well, I say "relationship", but probably there was never a true relationship. It was just me trying to satisfy her needs, regardless of how strange, incoherent, or even painful I might consider them. I did not care, I would have done anything to play by her rules, even lie, as long as it would buy me another chance of seeing her or hearing from her. It was wrong, and I never want to be in a situation like this again. I have a lot of work to do on myself to regain self-confidence and self-respect, to be able to listen to my soul and pursue my own needs. Pain, difficulties, and sacrifices can be tolerable, but there needs to be some light at the end of the tunnel. There was so little for me in what we had, and the pain and suffering I endured daily were just leading me to self-destruction.

For the past eight months I have been living every week waiting for the Saturday, the only day when I had a chance of meeting her for a few hours. Most times I was left there hanging until the very last moment before knowing if we would see each other. Meanwhile, I was just killing time, trying to distract myself from the nerve-racking wait for her messages. I have a lot of responsibilities in the establishing of this pattern. Why did she have me wait until late in the evening every time? I think it was because I had taught her that it was all right to do so, that I would run to her no matter what. I was too scared of losing her to be able to set my own rules on the relationship.

Only a week ago, while I was visiting my parents, she called me and expressed once more the wish that we should break up and never talk again. This left me devastated for the millionth time; I could not sleep at all that night and left for the airport the following morning feeling like a zombie. I liked that I had the strength not to reply to her messages. She needed to take responsibility for her decision. (Because it was her choice, and she knew I was not okay with it). But she didn't! She came to wait for me at the airport, and once more brought me closer to her. She now accuses me of having played with her! You know how often in the last few months I have felt like one of those little rubber bouncy balls? At one moment I am secure in the palm of her hand, just to be left falling to the floor one second later. And every time, she picks me up, holds on to me briefly, and then lets me fall from higher up.

When she threw her accusations at me two days ago, she started questioning whether she really knows me. Well, I don't know if she does. I don't even know how well I know myself. Maybe being caught up in this toxic vortex exposed a lot of weaknesses that I did not know I had, so in a sense I understand myself better. On the other hand, I was just trying to be what she wanted me to be, the best that I could be for her, although there was no clear path to follow. Could that behavior help in finding out who I really am? Probably not. It just raised further questions.

I gave her eight months of my life. I was hers in the most literal sense, held by invisible but powerful chains. In a twisted way, I find it almost funny that everything is ending because she thinks I cheated on her. In my mind this is the most ludicrous charge that can be brought against me. Does she really think that? She has made similar accusations against me before. But it doesn't matter. Maybe it is for the best that she believes it. I know in the back of my mind that I needed to break away from Jessica. I had been thinking about it a lot in the last few days. But I also appreciate how hard it would have been for me to take a step in that direction, given how chained to her I was. Now she has broken those chains for me, and I need to run away. I never want to see her again.

I hope that she will be able to fix her issues, whatever they are. I hope that she will overcome her fear of opening up to people and will experience healthy and positive love in the future. I truly hope that for her. As for me, I still need to shake off this belief that I can make this relationship work just by pure willpower. It will take time. Those few moments of unbelievable elation came at a high price, a price that I am still paying. Such crazy rides are not what love is about, at least not for me.

I am trying to speak rationally, but I am also in tears. Part of me does not want to accept what I just said, and still wants to believe that we can be together. Does she love me truly? How can I help her and at the same time help myself? What could I have done differently to make this relationship work?

Questions for you

- What words of encouragement would you say to Martin as he tries to put his life back together?
- Martin described several red flags that appeared early on in the relationship. Which of these particularly stick out to you?
- Is it ever acceptable for a partner to go for days ignoring their significant other? Should this sort of behavior be an automatic deal-breaker?
- Martin talks about telling seemingly insignificant "white lies" to Jessica in order to prevent himself from being put into an even more vulnerable position. Do you think this is justified in certain circumstances? Or does it further perpetuate the opaque and dishonest nature of the relationship?
- Do you think that Jessica is a bad person for behaving in this way? Or are her own inner demons contributing to her behavior? Even if that is the case, at what stage should someone be held responsible for their own actions, regardless of whether or not they suffer from a personality disorder? What advice would you give to her?

3

The Story of Amanda and Chris

Amanda and Chris are a couple in their late thirties and have been together for two and a half years. They met through mutual friends, and both live in the same metropolitan area where their families are rooted. Amanda works in retail, while Chris is currently unemployed – having been laid-off from his bartending job when the COVID-19 pandemic broke out. They moved in together a few months before Chris lost his job, and since then the relationship has gone through many difficult changes.

Relatively early on, Chris revealed to Amanda that he had been diagnosed with a condition called Borderline Personality Disorder, but that he was able to manage the symptoms with the help of his therapist. Shortly after losing his job though, he abruptly quit his therapy sessions making the excuse that he had no desire to continue with them in the new virtual format that was necessary due to the worldwide Coronavirus pandemic. Amanda then started to document several disconcerting trends in Chris's behavior.

His general state of mind became erratic and unpredictable, sometimes undergoing several mood swings in a single day. He also grew much more possessive, developing an extreme sense of paranoia around whom Amanda was spending her time with when they were not together. His interests shifted, becoming increasingly focused on their relationship and losing almost all drive for his former hobbies and activities. Amanda, on the other hand, still had many external interests and activities, but Chris started to make her feel guilty for taking part in them.

Perhaps the most startling new development she noticed in their relationship was that Chris would often give a distorted recount of fights and arguments that they had had. He would present things as the exact opposite of the way she remembered them taking place. At first, she thought he was misremembering or perhaps just lying, but after repeated exposure to such behavior, she eventually started to question her own memories of these events.

Worried that the relationship was falling apart, and now less able to trust her own thoughts and memories, Amanda started her own therapy sessions. She tells us her story below:

I felt a deep connection with Chris very early on in our relationship. I had never met anyone who made me feel so unique, so special. He seemed to know me better than anyone else – it was as if he could read my thoughts and my feelings. He'd frequently flatter me and buy me nice gifts, sometimes totally out of the blue. But he'd also occasionally say things that would make me uncomfortable, like "I can't believe that I'm so lucky to be dating you. You're so far out of my league." and "If I ever lost you, I don't know if I could go on." At first, I wrote this off to what I perceived to be his over-exaggerated and self-deprecating charm. Now I feel that these were actually the first of many red flags indicating his underlying struggles.

A few months into our relationship, he told me that he had previously been diagnosed with Borderline Personality Disorder. I knew that he was going to therapy twice a month, but up until that point I had never asked him the details. While I had heard of BPD before, I really didn't know much about it. He told me that he used to have terrible mood swings and that he had also struggled to maintain a fixed personality. Thankfully, he had been able to manage his symptoms with the help of his therapist. I started to read more about BPD and began to see more of these traits subtly emerge in our relationship.

The situation precipitated when Coronavirus hit, and Chris lost his job. While a degree of depression and disappointment for anyone in these circumstances is totally understandable, he reacted in probably the worst way possible: he quit going to his therapy sessions! Since then, things have taken a sharp turn for the worse in our relationship. I've noticed more and more ups and downs in his behavior, more mood swings. One moment we'll be head-over-heels in love, and in the next, the littlest thing could send him into a tailspin! Sometimes he'll be triggered by a misinterpreted, playful comment I make, while at other times he'll be set off by something that he completely imagines. But whatever the root cause, the common theme in these outbursts is that he feels personally attacked and seems to think that I'm intentionally sabotaging his self-esteem. I feel so guilty when this happens, and I've been absolutely powerless in getting him to see that I'm trying to do nothing of the sort. In reality, he's the one who is sabotaging my mental well-being, but I don't know how to even broach this subject with him lest I risk an even bigger explosion.

In the past, he always had good people skills – even if his outgoing persona was somewhat of an act. But after being stuck at home, day after day, without his usual therapy sessions to keep him in check, he's became very possessive and jealous whenever I spend time with anyone other than him. I can understand why he is bitter about his situation, but I don't understand why he has shifted all his negative feelings onto me. He's started accusing me of cheating or of wanting to leave him. As he's become more of a recluse, he's started to expect me to do so as well. He told me that he no longer trusts our mutual friends, because he thinks they are trying to pry into our relationship. He even told me that he disapproves of me talking to my mother and sister. Here is the mysterious part that I don't yet understand: while this controlling behavior would have pushed me away in any previous relationship, it has had the opposite effect here. The more he criticizes me, the more I wonder whether I deserve it! I know this is unhealthy, but I'm finding it more and more difficult to put up resistance.

He repeatedly tells me that I'm at the center of his universe – his everything – but I've found that this has become increasingly true for me as well. We are completely dependent on one other, and I've given him full control to dictate the tone of our relationship. Before I do anything these days I play out the scenarios in my mind of how he is going to react. But he can be so unpredictable that no amount of pre-planning can stave off one of his outbursts. One thing that really bothers me is that he makes up his own version of events after they take place. At first, I thought he was either lying or else just had a terrible memory. But after this happened enough times, I started to question my own memories! It's a frightening thing not to know whether the things you remember actually took place or not. But I'm afraid to even bring up this issue with him.

Don't get me wrong – we still have moments when he makes me feel like the most special person in the world. Just a few days ago he surprised me with flowers and took me to the park where we had our first date. These are the sort of moments I live for, the sorts of memories that keep me coming back to him even after I endure his psychological abuse. But then at other times we have mild disagreements that quickly spiral into painful screaming matches. One tactic he uses during our fights is really brilliant when you understand it (and I do not know if he does it consciously or not). He cycles between attacking me (which I expect) and attacking himself (which is much more difficult to endure). One minute he is calling me names, but then in the next he tells me that he knows he's a loser, and that I'd be better off if he didn't exist. I'm then left trying to convince him that this isn't true and that he means the world to me.

Maybe I should give in to his demands and focus more of my time on him. If something ever happened to Chris, I wouldn't be able to forgive myself. I know he needs to go back to therapy, but he's now fully convinced that it was always a waste of time and never did him any good. At the moment, I'm focusing on the only thing I can do to save our relationship: change myself into the person that he wants me to be.

Questions for you

- Chris was aware of his Borderline Personality Disorder and was seeing a therapist before the relationship started. It was after he quit therapy that his symptoms re-emerged. In what ways is Chris's situation different from someone who has never been diagnosed with BPD before?
- How much is Amanda and Chris's situation due to external

circumstances like the global pandemic? What would have been different if Chris had kept going to therapy?

- Do you think Amanda's focus of changing herself into the person that she perceives Chris wants her to be is healthy? What should she focus on instead?
- Can the relationship between Amanda and Chris improve, and if so, how?

4

Lessons from the Stories

What makes the stories of Martin and Amanda similar? They both experienced a romantic relationship with a partner whose personality has Borderline traits. In one case there was an actual diagnosis of Borderline Personality Disorder. While it can be crystal clear that something is wrong in a relationship, it might be much more difficult to have an unequivocal picture of the situation, to understand precisely where the problems lie, and to know whether it is possible to fix them. Often one is left confused, ruminating over questions like those that were asked at the end of the two previous stories. This book was written to help you find the answers to those questions and to devise an appropriate course of action.

If your relationship is stuck in a cycle of repeated dysfunction or any of the situations described in the stories above sound familiar, it is possible that your partner suffers from Borderline Personality Disorder. We understand the difficulties of your situation, and would like to give you a chance to improve your life. We want you to realize that you are not going crazy, and you should not blame yourself for the hardships you have been experiencing. Our first aim is to give you tools to understand your partner's behavior and make an honest assessment of your relationship. But we will not stop there. Our ultimate goal is to provide not only a theoretical understanding but also concrete advice on how to manage your relationship. Is it worth continuing or should you end it? We will help you make that choice. Regardless of whether you decide to stay in the relationship or to leave it, we give practical advice on how to pursue your choice in the most effective and successful way. The message of this book will be summarized in an eight-step process, which you should frequently refer to throughout your recovery.

To solve a problem, it is important to correctly identify its true causes. Your partner's personality disorder is at the root of the issues that you experience in your relationship. But we are not trying to assign blame. This book makes it clear the unhealthy behaviors of a person with BPD are not part of their true self: the most negative traits are just symptoms of their personality disorder.

In the next part of this book we dive deep into BPD, describing the most common traits of this personality disorder as well as its causes and the factors that lead to its persistence. The remaining two parts of the book are addressed more directly to you. In particular, you will become more aware of your suffering and of the ways in which your unhealthy relationship has affected you. Understanding your situation will be the starting point to make lasting improvements to your life.

II

UNDERSTANDING BPD

5

The Traits of a Borderline Personality

Borderline Personality Disorder (BPD) is a serious medical condition, and as such can only be diagnosed by a professional. However, we have a right to personally evaluate a situation around us and act accordingly. If we know that a friend is less than likely to pay off their debts, we understand that lending them money is a bad idea without having to see their official credit score. Likewise, there is no need to wait for our partner to be diagnosed with BPD by a professional before we start changing our own behavior in relation to them. The longer we wait to take action, the harder the consequences may be.

In this chapter we will answer the question: *What are the common traits and symptoms of Borderline Personality Disorder?* Broadly speaking, BPD is characterized by insecurity and emotional distress. People with BPD experience inconsistencies in their feelings, thoughts, relationships, identity, and actions. They travel through life on an emotional roller coaster, where ups can change to downs in little more than the blink of an eye. As a result, their personal relationships can be highly tumultuous and unstable. An overwhelming sense of insecurity and a fear of being discarded will often coexist alongside extreme outbursts of personality. These can be fits of rage, or an impulsive drive to engage in self-destructive behaviors. When people with BPD are distressed, they are more likely to act without thinking, and might threaten self-harm or even attempt suicide. Borderline people often suffer from depression, and have a hard time finding out who they are and what they want in life. Therefore, it is often difficult for them to pursue long term projects or to fully commit to anything, whether it is a job or a personal relationship. They are also prone to struggle with self-confidence and have poor physical and emotional balance. In summary, people suffering from BPD have a hard time making straightforward life decisions and staying grounded in reality.

We will now discuss Borderline traits in detail. Keep in mind that around 2% of the population meets the diagnostic requirements for BPD – by no means a small number of people. However, there are *many more* people who may have not been tested, yet share many of the central characteristics of this disorder. While only a trained professional can make an official diagnosis of BPD, we will focus our attention here on dealing with loved ones who exhibit *Borderline traits*. This book was written to equip you with tools to better understand these people, and to prepare you to make difficult yet necessary decisions that will ultimately improve your life.

Dysregulation of Emotions

Emotional dysregulation broadly refers to a lack of emotional control. People with BPD have a hard time managing their feelings and are often overwhelmed by them. We all have moments when we experience extreme emotion – whether we are extraordinarily happy, angry, annoyed, or even just bored to death. A well-centered person has the ability to keep their feelings in check and to avoid many of the adverse effects of out-of-control emotions. This is a key component of a stable life – most of the time we manage to carry on our daily routine without being excessively influenced by the goings on of our inner self. But for a person with BPD traits, maintaining a healthy balance of emotions proves to be difficult, if not outright impossible. To them, each feeling acts like a raging river swelling out of nowhere and is often immediately followed by erratic and impulsive behavioral patterns. Emotional dysregulation is one of the central problems that people with BPD face.

"My girlfriend and I have been together for several months. While much of our relationship has been great, sometimes the littlest things will make her fly off the handle. She recently got a haircut that I find attractive, and I told her that I like it. She then got really defensive and accused me of not liking her haircut because, according to her reasoning, the fact that I said that I like it means that I secretly don't like it and that I felt the need to disguise my dislike with a compliment! What am I supposed to do? Say nothing? My innocent comment snowballed into a big argument, and I was powerless to calm her down. These types of outbursts are becoming more and more frequent and I'm wondering if our relationship can be fixed."

Unstable Moods

As we have just seen, people suffering from BPD have a hard time regulating their emotions and preventing inner struggles from interfering with their daily activities. In addition, they are easily triggered by their environment into experiencing unusually strong feelings. BPD sufferers can have intense and extreme reactions to circumstances that do not affect others in the same way. They are more easily upset by what others say or do and are more prone to feeling extreme levels of stress. Even a mildly critical comment or a disapproving glance can send a person with BPD into an emotional tailspin. Because a person suffering from BPD may have an extreme response even to a small and seemingly insignificant event, their emotions can fluctuate wildly. They can be exuberant one minute and an absolute wreck the next. These unpredictable mood swings, coupled with the extreme way in which their emotions are expressed, can make living around a person with Borderline Personality Disorder extremely difficult.

Problems with Anger Management

Another symptom of BPD is a difficulty in controlling rage. Many seemingly innocuous behaviors or circumstances may irritate or anger someone with BPD. They can be triggered by the ticking of a clock, by someone doodling on a piece of paper, by an open door, or by a towel not being positioned in the right way. They can get mad at you for not responding promptly to their call, or because the chocolate you bought is not their favorite brand, or because you were "too nice" to someone else. The person suffering from BPD may misinterpret these behaviors as betrayal and become angry about them. *"If you had cared enough about me, you would have known better than to do such a thing!"* When overcome by intense anger, they can lose control by throwing objects, by screaming at you, or even by suddenly feeling so overwhelmed that they simply cannot decide how to respond. After each such rageful episode, they will often experience shame, depression, and remorse – which can then be every bit as challenging to deal with as the rage outburst itself (both for the person with BPD and those around them). Some people suffering from BPD will spend a significant amount of time blaming themselves for these events and turning their anger inwards. Episodes of rage directed towards oneself can result in extremely destructive behavior and self-harm, as we will see below.

Dysregulation of Interpersonal Relationships

Interpersonal dysregulation is characterized by difficulties in forming and maintaining relationships with others. This does not mean that people with Borderline Personality Disorder are generally unpleasant or unlikeable. They can at times be fascinating and sensitive, charming and engaging. Nonetheless, most external observers are typically put off by their erratic behaviors and mood swings. Finding BPD sufferers so hard to please and to understand, people are often discouraged from engaging in deeper relationships. This difficulty to keep and grow friendships fuels negative feelings and insecurities that are already present in the people with BPD. They consider themselves to be unworthy of attention or love and feel that they will eventually be abandoned by those around them.

Intense but Unstable Romantic Relationships

Given the instability of their internal feelings, it comes as no surprise that people with BPD tend to have tumultuous, out-of-control romantic relationships. Their lack of emotional strength makes it difficult – if not impossible – for them to effectively cope with the common challenges faced by couples. If you are in a relationship with someone who suffers from BPD, you will notice that sometimes the relationship is going wonderfully, and then at other times things go completely off the rails. At one moment you find yourself happy and excited, thrilled and confident about your future together, while the next moment you are filled with hopeless thoughts about what may happen next. The cause of this erratic emotional whiplash that you feel is the internal turmoil and uncertainties that characterize the constant struggle of the person living with BPD. Their relationships, like their feelings, seem to be on a roller coaster, alternating back and forth between the extremely good and the extremely bad. This makes romantic relationships difficult to manage. Since they themselves do not know what they really want, your same behavior can be seen favorably today and shamed tomorrow. Whatever you say or do can trigger an unpredictable reaction. One day you might bring home a cake, to your partner's delight. But if you do it again a week later, their reaction could be completely different. *"Why do you want me to eat all this sweet stuff? You obviously do not care about my health! You must hate me!"* A relationship with a Borderline partner can be intensely satisfying during the good times, but in the bad times it can be plagued by arguments, screaming matches, and even physical violence.

Intense Efforts to Prevent Abandonment

Fear of being left alone is one of the most severe issues for people suffering from BPD. When their relationship with a friend, romantic partner, family member, or therapist either ends or significantly changes, the person suffering from BPD feels panicked and scared. Since their inner life is so unstable and insecure, they are prone to look for reassurance and confirmation in the people around them, and consequently, have a hard time letting go. They believe that the people in their life are unique and irreplaceable and, if they lose them, they will be alone for the rest of their lives and not receive the help they need to overcome their everyday struggles. The fear of being deserted and remaining isolated can be so debilitating that some people with BPD will go to extreme lengths to keep others from abandoning them. They might beg and plead, attempt to start a fight, or resort to hurtful emotional blackmail, trying to make the other person feel guilty about leaving. They can even threaten to cause physical harm, both to others and to themselves. In extreme cases, BPD sufferers have such a fear of being deserted that they may even attempt suicide in a way to try and prevent abandonment.

"I have no doubt that my boyfriend loves me, but he has serious difficulties with trust, and this is really starting to grate on our relationship. He told me that he doesn't like me hanging out with my guy friends, because he thinks that if I do, I'll inevitably leave him for one of them. You know what? The more he acts like this, the more likely he'll be proven right. But he has thrown such outrageous tantrums when I have threatened to leave him that I'm now quite scared to do so. Once he started punching himself in the chin and

even bashed his head into the wall. Then he blamed me for making him hurt himself! Please give me advice! I just don't know how to de-escalate this situation."

Behavioral Dysregulation and Impulsivity

People suffering from BPD often engage in out-of-control behaviors that can have a negative impact on their life. Sometimes they are completely unable to exercise any restraint and will act on the spur of the moment, regardless of consequences. To an outside observer, it appears that they are not in control of their own actions. Overwhelmed by their feelings, they might say something hurtful and offensive, write a nasty comment on Facebook, become violent, or engage in inappropriate behavior at work that puts them at risk of being fired. Sometimes this lack of restraint leads to even more dangerous circumstances. People with BPD can take risks that could hurt themselves or others, for instance, driving recklessly or engaging in risky sexual behavior. Other examples of behavioral dysregulation are impulsive spending, binge eating, or drug and alcohol abuse. People with BPD often faced many, if not all, of these problems at some point in their life. While they may consciously understand that these habits are harmful to their health and impair their social interactions, they still engage in them. They impulsively give in to such instincts, mainly when angry and frustrated, in an attempt to temporarily relieve their emotional pain.

Self-Destructive or Suicidal Behavior

When people with BPD become aware of the effects of their impulsive and reckless behaviors, they can be led into even more extreme actions, instead of reconsidering and retracing their steps. Such extremes often involve deliberately hurting oneself and contemplating suicide. Self-harm and suicide threats are also used to blackmail people into not walking away from them. Remember that one of their greatest fear is being left alone. If a loved one threatens self-harm or suicide, you should seek help immediately.

Uncertainty about One's Personality

The underlying cause of many of the behaviors described so far is the shaky sense of self that characterizes people with BPD. They lack a strong personal identity and their perception of who they are will change dramatically depending on the situation. In different contexts, it is natural for everyone to feel and behave differently. Certainly, when we are at home, we do not talk the same way that we talk at work. We do not behave the same way when we play with our children as we do when we are out with friends. People with Borderline Personality Disorder, however, not only behave differently in various circumstances, but they often seem to become an entirely different person each time. They lack those strong unifying features that define a distinct "personality". They do not know who they really are, and because of this lack of identity, their character traits are extremely volatile. When you are dealing with a Borderline person you quickly realize that they are totally unpredictable. Even if you think you know them, you might find yourself surprised by their behavior at any time. Their lack of a concrete identity and purpose often leads to frequent and extreme life changes: they change jobs, partners, homes, cities, friends. If you look closely, they have no solid idea of who they are or where they are going in life.

Feelings of Emptiness

A consequence of the lack of a solid identity is a constant sense of emptiness. People with BPD tend to feel hollow, like an empty shell – as if they had a big hole inside that they do not know how to fill. Many of them would use the words "nothing" or "nobody" to describe themselves. The search for this missing part of themselves is what drives many of their actions. Unfortunately, we are not merely talking about a small missing piece of a puzzle, the shape and details of which can be inferred from the surrounding environment. A significant portion of their personality is missing and, as we saw above, this creates a sense of instability that is reflected in each of their behaviors.

Suspicious Thoughts

One of the most distinctive traits of a Borderline personality is having constant suspicions or paranoid thoughts, especially about the actions of others. It is not necessary to be delusional, schizophrenic, or psychotic to struggle with such a problem. Borderline people worry about how others perceive them and tend to constantly see signs around them that reinforce the negative feelings they have about themselves. For example, they may assume that people make fun of them *"He is thinking I am fat, look how he is staring at me, he definitely hates me."* They tend to overreact to the smallest signs. Even when someone is nice to them, they become highly suspicious, questioning their motives and good faith. Their basic assumption is that other people are trying to be cruel to them, to belittle, exploit, or take advantage of them in some way.

6

Life's Misfortunes: The Causes of BPD

If you have picked up this book, you probably care deeply for someone whose personality has Borderline traits. Even when you feel trapped by such a person and their destructive attitudes and behaviors, you should keep in mind that they are not evil monsters. They are not necessarily behaving this way on purpose. They may well have nothing against you personally, and they are probably not spending all their waking moments trying to get even with you. There are many reasons, of course, underlying their often-unpredictable conduct, and most of the time those have nothing to do with you. So, what are these reasons then? Well, the words and actions of a BPD sufferer can only be understood and evaluated in the context of their condition. Thus, asking the motives of their behaviors is much like asking the causes of BPD, which is the topic of this section.

Borderline Personality Disorder is a complicated condition, and therefore it is not surprising that its causes are diverse and complex. Although there is no single trait or event that can be held responsible for causing this disorder, several factors have been identified which make it more likely that a person will suffer from BPD. Some of these factors are present in genetics, while others are linked to life experiences. Before discussing them in detail, it is worth spelling out the main message of this section: *You should keep in mind that a person with Borderline Personality Disorder has often had a difficult and complicated past. If you find it a worthwhile endeavor to understand their thought processes and see the world through their eyes, you have no choice but to get acquainted and engage with their past experiences.*

You have undoubtedly heard of the *nature vs. nurture* controversy, which concerns whether the individual characteristics of a human being are caused by hard-wired genetic influences that are present when we are born (nature) or by our environment (nurture). To be frank, this discussion has been happening for years, and we are no closer to answering it now than when the question was first raised. There is a general agreement that both nature and nurture play a role in all psychiatric disorders. While it is true that there is a genetic component to BPD, we know that life experience is a major determining factor in bringing out these genetic predispositions. We will focus on such real-life triggers, as they are there the only ones that we can examine and identify with certainty. While it is difficult if not impossible to investigate our genetic structure, it is far easier to look back on our past and consider all the traumas we have experienced and how we felt in those moments. Talking about life experiences and revisiting the past is indeed the starting point of any therapy. Furthermore, the real-life setting, as opposed to our genetics, is the only one that is under our control and where we can try to make changes.

In this section we will discuss the environmental factors that are more likely to lead to BDP. As you will see, they provide some sort of rational explanation for the previously described traits of a Borderline personality.

Childhood Maltreatment and Traumatic Experiences

Childhood maltreatment is among the most important environmental factors related to BPD. With this term we mean any form of violation that is inflicted on children. It encompasses all types of physical and emotional mistreatment, ranging from being ignored, unsupported or neglected to being subjected to physical or sexual abuse. Within this broad spectrum, most people suffering from BPD have undergone some sort of severe maltreatment as children.

The origins of many of the characteristics of a borderline personality can be traced back to previous traumatic experiences. In particular, the erratic behaviors of the people with BPD that may not make sense at first, acquire some meaning considering the abuse that they endured as children. We elaborate on this point in the following paragraphs.

We have seen how people with BPD suffer from emotional instability and have a hard time establishing healthy relationships with other people. Such problems can be attributed to a common denominator of many different traumatic experiences, which at any time are capable of triggering the process of *dissociation*. During an episode of dissociation, your body and mind shut down and stop processing information.

A person experiencing dissociation feels disconnected from their own thoughts and memories. It is as if the body and mind have temporarily shut down and are now completely numb. The flow of information coming in from the outside world is interrupted, thus making the person detached from their surroundings. Through dissociation, people stop feeling emotions and being impacted by what is happening around them. Dissociation is therefore a defense mechanism that provides temporary relief from physical and emotional distress during a traumatic experience. It makes any form of abuse a little more bearable. In the long run, however, when it is experienced frequently, it can turn into a habit that manifests itself without any definitive triggering factor.

Dissociation provides a safe space. It is a natural and appropriate defense when we are powerless children, and our mind needs a corner to hide in, where it can feel safe and ignore the bad things that are happening around us. Problems arise when adults maintain this habit of seeking a mental escape rather than dealing with the complexities of real life. Many people who suffered from abuse cannot give up on such behavior even though they are now in a different position, no longer the same helpless victims of circumstances that they were as children. In people with BPD, dissociation is a persistent event, which continues to occur even when the traumatic experiences from childhood are far in the past. These people may have become so used to the trauma that they see it everywhere around them and react the only way they are used to. Every little experience can be seen by them as traumatic and therefore a trigger for dissociation.

Frequent dissociation in people with BPD affects their perception of inner life, their sense of identity and the understanding of their own feelings. It also causes them to be less receptive to signals from the outside as their information flow is intermittent and inconsistent. Episodes of dissociation can create a very confusing picture of the world in their mind, thus making it extremely difficult for them to have healthy interactions with others.

We have already explained that a paranoid level of suspicion is a cognitive symptom of BPD. Borderline people have a hard time trusting others and live with the constant feeling that other people have a negative opinion of them. If you suffered from neglect or abuse as a child, it is no surprise that you developed such a wary attitude. Fears of rejection and abandonment, and rocky and chaotic relationships can also be explained in a similar way. Being abused as a child makes it difficult to feel secure in relationships with others later in life, especially if the abuser was someone very close, such as a mother, father, or caregiver. People with a Borderline personality may have already experienced severe betrayal from a person who was supposed to take care of them, treat them well, stand by them and support them. From this viewpoint, it is natural for them to ask whether they can ever trust anyone again.

Remember that these are typically not considerations carried out through conscious reasoning. BPD sufferers do not sit there and ask themselves *"Can I trust this person, based on my previous life experiences?"*, let alone answer that question rationally. All these processes occur at a subconscious level. *People with BPD may be largely unaware of the deep reasons behind their actions and are often in denial of their biases and of the far-reaching effects of their disquieting past.*

The mistrust displayed by people with BPD is an involuntary emotional response. It comes from the way their instinct has been trained to react after years and years of enduring the same traumatic experience. Skepticism and suspiciousness constitute mechanisms of self-defense that remain active well after the initial abuse that triggered them in the first place has disappeared. Unfortunately, when deployed in an environment that is no longer hostile, they make it difficult if not impossible to live healthy personal relationships.

Misgiving, suspiciousness, and fear of being deserted are built inside the person with BDP, and they need to be eradicated in the same way in which the operating system of a computer is reprogrammed. Such a result can be only achieved through a long and difficult therapy process. You can talk to BPD sufferers and try to battle their negative core believes with rational arguments, but that will not work. Your encouraging and sensible words will not change their deeply grounded convictions and will likely not even suffice to make them rethink their attitude.

It is not uncommon for people with BPD to experience self-harm tendencies and suicidal thoughts. Unsurprisingly, these traits are generally related to serious mistreatment during childhood, such as sexual abuse. These horrifying experiences left them feeling not only betrayed but also worthless, as if their life were meaningless. Often BPD people have experienced their first suicidal thoughts already as children or teenagers.

"My wife and I have had a significant amount of difficulties during most of the six years we've been married. Our marriage was frequently caught up in fights over little things that didn't matter, and at the time, I largely blamed this on her erratic personality. I looked at the situation as if she was acting this way on purpose, and I never made an effort to ask why she was so unstable. Our sex life would go through periods of being wild and wonderful, to other long stretches in which she'd show no interest in sex at all. Worried about our relationship, I convinced her to start attending couples therapy with me. It was there that she revealed that she had had several affairs since we had been married. I was shocked and furious. She was bawling when she admitted this to me, but before I had time to even fully process this information, she also revealed that she had been sexually abused as a teenager. All of a sudden, her volatile behavior made more sense. I still love my wife, despite the betrayal that I feel from her. She is now seeking in-patient treatment and I'm doing everything in my power to forgive her and start fresh. But it's so hard, and I'm not sure if I'm strong enough to do it."

Environments that are Invalidating

There are other childhood experiences, apart from actual violence, that may also contribute to Borderline Personality Disorder. Growing up in an invalidating setting is one of them. To invalidate something means saying that it is not natural, genuine, understandable, or accurate. In this context we are typically going to be referring to parents invalidating the feelings and emotions experienced by their children.

Here are some simple examples of what it means to spend your childhood in an invalidating environment.

You are really excited about the good result of a school test, and you are looking forward to celebrating with your parents. Unfortunately, your mom appears to react coldly to the news, and she quickly extinguishes your enthusiasm: *"There is nothing to be happy about, you just did what was expected of you".*

You feel sad because you had a fight with one of your best friends, where you ended up calling each other names. You are extremely upset about this episode, but your dad is dismissive: *"Come on, be a man and stop crying".*

You are on holiday with your parents and your dad challenges you to jump into the water from a high rock. When you finally make it, after a little hesitation, your father says: *"Good job! Do you see now that there was no need to be afraid, and you were just being a crybaby?"* Your mom reinforces the message: *"You see how easy it was? It was silly of you to be scared".*

You have just learned to tie your shoes, but your parents are not as proud as you would have expected: *"It was about time you learned, even dumb people can do it".*

You are angry at your father because he forgot that you were finishing school early today, and he came to pick you up one hour late. In the car he tries to downplay the situation: *"Come on, you are not really angry, I know that you are just pretending".*

Each of these episodes considered by itself seems innocuous enough, but a repeated exposure to attitudes of this kind can have serious long-term effects. In all these examples the foundation or the reality of the child's feelings is questioned or attacked. This can be done in different ways by denying, ridiculing, ignoring, or judging the emotions that have been expressed. Regardless of the means, the message is clear: your feelings are *wrong*! You had no grounds for experiencing and showing happiness, sadness, fear, pride, or anger. Your emotions were unjustified and had no reason to be displayed or even exist.

Invalidation can be considered a form of abuse, although it is much more subtle than the mistreatment discussed in the previous section. It is a process that can go on undetected for a long time, with both the victims and even the perpetrators potentially being unaware of it. With violent abuse, children often know that something negative is happening to them. The same cannot be said regarding invalidation, which, as we have seen in the third example above, can even be disguised as a praise.

For children, receiving feedback that reflects how they think or feel about themselves and the world around them is important and reassuring – it validates their experiences and helps them build up their inner self. Hearing something that completely contradicts their perception, on the other hand, can be upsetting and disturbing. *"Can't I be sad after fighting with my best friend?" "I thought being afraid of jumping into the water from thirty feet high was normal, or at least understandable. Apparently, I was wrong: it was totally unreasonable and unrelatable."* Children tend to seek positive reinforcements from the people that they are closest to, especially their parents. When they receive invalidation instead of encouragement, doubts and confusion begin to make their way into their personalities.

When a child's perceptions are constantly questioned and challenged, they start believing that something is wrong with their emotions and that they should not be experiencing such feelings in the first place. While growing up, they develop

- Mistrust of their own perceptions.
- Fear of their feelings and discomfort in expressing them.
- Repression of their emotions, which they think are wrong and unjustified.

People who grow up in an invalidating environment tend to become more and more uncomfortable with their internal feelings as time goes on. They often chastise themselves for being too emotional. They try to suppress their feelings until this suppression is no longer sustainable, at which point their emotions explode, suddenly letting everything out. This in turn triggers a new episode of self-punishment since they feel ashamed of that extreme display of emotion. Such vicious cycle keeps repeating itself and eventually becomes a mainstay of that person's interactions with the world.

There is another way in which invalidation can affect the management of a person's feelings. Let us consider for instance the second of the examples at the beginning of this section. A child has just received an invalidating message from his father after expressing sadness. What should he do? He could try voicing his sadness more forcefully in the attempt to persuade his father that his feelings are real. Maybe he will do that for a few times. But in the end, he will learn *"I must not cry in front of dad or he will get mad".* The child will therefore start to hide his sadness to his father. On the other hand, he might compensate by crying twice as hard with his grandmother, knowing that he can expect from her an empathic response. In this way a pattern of extreme inconsistency is established: a cover up is followed by an intense outburst of emotions. These ups and downs can become permanent, just the "normal" way of dealing with one's inner life, the way that was learned during childhood and that now one is unable to leave behind. In the most extreme cases the result of this inability is a full-blown personality disorder. We have seen in fact how people with BPD constantly alternate between suffocating their emotions and exploding, expressing them forcefully.

Here is the bottom line of this section: *The most prominent characteristics of BPD, which involve trouble in controlling emotions, are often the outcome of growing up in an invalidating environment. Being constantly told that one's feelings are not correct or legitimate encourages a person to avoid emotions at all costs, and feelings can appear frightening and unmanageable as a result.*

Factors that Lead to the Persistence of BPD

We have examined in the previous section several environmental circumstances that might cause Borderline Personality Disorder. It is also essential, however, to understand what types of factors can help sustain BPD over time. Chaos and adversity in life are definitely among these factors. People with BPD usually face a considerable number of uncomfortable, stressful incidents and hassles. They might have lost their job, a family member, or a loved one, they might have been involved in a severe car accident, they might have been abandoned by an intimate partner, publicly humiliated, or endured other similar setbacks. The expression *"unrelenting crisis"* can be used to describe people with BPD's proclivity for experiencing many highly stressful events. They become convinced that their life's crises will never end and will just keep on coming, one after the other, with no respite for them to recover or prepare for the next disaster.

What forms of stress do people with BPD feel the most? Conflict with others is perhaps the most common cause of anxiety, and it constitutes a frequent trigger of self-harm and suicidal behavior. Other important causes of emotional distress are being rejected, failing at something, and being left alone.

Being constantly exposed to stressful life events can worsen the problems that people with BPD face. They already have a hard time finding an emotional balance within themselves, and additional upsetting circumstances in their daily life make them even more frustrated and vulnerable. They cannot cope with such occurrences, because of their instability and their feeling of lacking the right tools to get through life. In general, people who are upset are more prone to act on instinct and engage in potentially harmful behaviors. This is true for everyone. When we are angry, we are more likely to behave rashly, seeking some way to relieve our stress and pain. People who are lifting heavy weights are more likely to drop them when a new weight is added or when they are tired from doing multiple repetitions. Similarly, if someone is continually confronted with disquieting events, and is already hurt from past traumatic experienced (as is often the case with BPD sufferers), their coping mechanisms can be exhausted to the point that they resort to extreme behaviors, such as self-harm and substance abuse.

This brings us to another aspect that can contribute to the persistence of BPD: many of the habits associated with it have an addictive or compulsive component to them. We have already seen that one of the characteristics of BPD is behavioral dysregulation, which involves impulsive habits including binge eating, unsafe sex, drug and alcohol abuse, reckless driving, suicide attempts, self-harm, etc. The problem with all these behaviors is that they do make people feel better, at least temporarily. They are somehow effective in giving ephemeral relief from the stress and pain that the person with BPD is experiencing in a moment of crisis.

Psychologists use the word *reinforcement* to describe any effect that makes someone more likely to repeat a behavior in a similar situation. For example, if getting drunk after fighting with your partner makes you feel better for a short time, then you will be more likely to drink again when your partner criticizes you in the future. The relief that you experience reinforces your drinking. Many of the patterns associated with BPD work in this way: using drugs, hurting yourself, taking risks, but even more simply shouting at someone. Getting verbally abusive and throwing a tantrum can cause a temporary euphoria and provoke good mood or excitement.

We therefore understand how reinforcement fuels the vicious cycle in which BPD sufferers are trapped. As soon as they go through a traumatic experience (for example, being rejected by someone), they become emotionally distressed (they feel ashamed, sad, and maybe a little angry). This can happen to anyone, but people with BPD, because of their unstable internal emotions, find it particularly challenging to come up with effective coping mechanisms. As a result, they may turn to impulsive acts, verbal or physical aggression, isolation, alcohol, or self-harm. They may feel better for a short time, but such behaviors will not fill the void left by the rejection that triggered them and will only lead to new problems in the future. What are the plans for the next time they are feeling stressed? More than likely, they will indulge in the same unhealthy habits that made them find temporary relief the first time around.

7

Overcoming BPD: Can It Be Cured?

This is not a book about treating and curing BPD. However, if you are dealing with a loved one who suffers from this condition, it is important for you to be aware that treatments do exist. In particular, if you are in a relationship with a person suffering from BPD, in deciding whether you want to stay or leave, you should have a clear picture of the chances that your partner will overcome the disorder (provided, of course, that you can convince them to seek professional help).

Psychological therapy and medication are the two primary forms of treatment available for people with BPD. Both are administered by professionals over an extensive period of time. What are the chances of them being successful, and in what timeframe? While a few decades ago mental health practitioners used to assume that BPD was a chronic illness with a slight possibility of recovery, this belief was founded mainly on unproved assumptions and anecdotal evidence. More recently, researchers have conducted thorough scientific investigations on how this condition progresses over time, tracking many individuals with the disorder to see how and when they heal. The findings of the following long-term study give us reason to be optimistic: *Zanarini MC et al. The longitudinal course of borderline psychopathology: 6-year prospective follow-up of the phenomenology of borderline personality disorder. Am J Psychiatry. 2003 Feb; 160(2): 274-83.* In a nutshell, this research shows that long-held assumptions about BPD's persistence and incurability are incorrect. There is now a lot of evidence that, after six years, most people diagnosed with BPD will no longer meet the requirements for this condition (that is, they will be in remission).

Dr. Mary Zanarini and her colleagues tracked the progress of 290 patients that were diagnosed with BPD. They discovered that 35 percent of them met criteria for remission after two years. Furthermore, almost half of all patients (49%) met criteria for remission after four years, and after six years, the number was 69 percent. In fact, throughout the six-year study, 74 percent of the patients who started with BPD no longer met the requirements for BPD at some stage. Notably, the vast majority of people (94%) who had stopped meeting BPD requirements never met those criteria again during the remainder of the study. In other words, BPD only rarely would go away only to resurface later on. For most patients, it went away and did not come back.

It is important to observe that this was not a therapy review, that is, the study was not designed to look at the benefits of a specific treatment for BPD. Hence, although most patients continued to receive psychiatric care during the study, the types of treatment they received differed. Moreover, not all the patients underwent treatment for the entire six years: some of them were not even receiving medication. This is significant because it indicates that, even in the absence of a specific state-of-the-art treatment for BPD, many people with this condition can gradually improve over time.

According to the authors of this study *"These results suggest that symptomatic improvement is both common and stable, even among the most disturbed borderline patients, and that the symptomatic prognosis for most, but not all, severely ill borderline patients is better than previously recognized".*

In conclusion, BPD could be much more changeable than we ever imagined, contrary to the popular belief that it sticks to you like glue, or a tattoo that you cannot get rid of.

III

LOVING A BPD SUFFERER

8

Starting off on the Wrong Foot

It is important to note that while no two Borderline Personality Disorder sufferers exhibit the exact same symptoms, many specific behavioral patterns are frequently encountered. One of the most common traits of an individual with BPD is the tendency to get involved in highly tumultuous personal relationships. In what ways do these relationships differ from normal and healthy ones? Understanding such differences is the key to managing personal interactions with a Borderline loved one. While many of the typical traits of those unhealthy relationships follow the instability patterns described below, it is important to recognize that there are also broad variations of the ways in which these patterns manifest themselves. For instance, in some cases BPD symptoms emerge in a relatively short period of time, but in others, it takes months or even years for these problematic behaviors to fully reveal themselves. In nearly all cases, however, the symptoms ebb and flow: at one moment their partner is falsely led to believe that a corner has been turned, only to leave them all the more disheartened when the Borderline behaviors re-emerge.

In order to manage a tempestuous relationship with a Borderline partner, *realistic expectations must be held at all times.* This chapter will tell you exactly what you should expect from such relationships.

Vulnerability as Means of Control

A woman suffering from BPD will often first appear to be shy and fragile and may give off an aura of someone in need of a rescuer. She will resort to over-the-top flattery as she awaits her Knight in Shining Armor coming in on a horse to sweep her off her feet. Presenting herself as someone in need of protection, she will let you know repeatedly that you are there to guard her and keep her safe. You will soon develop a deep sense of compassion for her as a reaction to her displays of emotion, which appear to be authentic and genuine. She will tell you that others have acted insensitively toward her and that her trust has been compromised. But she will make it clear that there is something unique about you because you understand her like no one has ever done before.

With a man suffering from BPD the initial experience will not be much different. When you get to know him, he might discuss at length how unlucky he has been in his life. He might describe a difficult family situation, as well as failed past relationships. He will tell you how previous partners have betrayed him and cheated on him repeatedly, so that he now feels like he cannot trust anyone. You will be moved by his story, believing that he really needs your genuine affection and love. He will encourage this attitude, claiming to see special qualities in you and that "you are not like the others".

Here is the bottom line: be extremely wary of any tendency towards self-victimization in a person you are thinking of entering into a romantic partnership with, as this is often a telltale sign of someone exhibiting traits of Borderline Personality Disorder.

The dominant way in which a Borderline person flatters you, together with the weak and vulnerable persona they might initially display at first, can prove to be very enticing. Such people come off as seductive and irresistible to someone who does not know or understand the signs of BPD to watch out for. If you are not careful, you will likely feel exalted by their behavior – often to the point of awkwardness. Though not true in all cases, this attitude usually emerges quite early on in the relationship. All humans need to feel loved and wanted, and Borderline people can be exceptionally good at exploiting this natural instinct, both consciously and unconsciously. You may tell yourself that this person is a dream come true: here is someone who not only wants to listen to your thoughts, your feelings, and your suggestions, but also goes out of their way to make you the center of their attention. Once such an emotional connection has been established, it may begin to look as though you have discovered your soulmate. In most cases though, this feeling will be rather short-lived. You will soon start to witness behaviors that are incomprehensible to you, and you will find yourself perplexed over what is actually happening. The answer is that you are well on your way to an unhealthy and codependent relationship with someone exhibiting many of the traits of a personality disorder.

When you start a relationship with a Borderline person, you may feel at first as if you are sailing the calm and secure waters of a familiar lake. You let your guard down and drift into a comfortable sleep, only to wake and find that your boat has drifted into the midst of an ocean monsoon, where you are throttled by the violent and relentless waves. If you experience this feeling in your relationship, then chances are that you have been sucked into your partner's cycle of *Idealization and Devaluation.* This is a common behavioral pattern that occurs in people suffering from Borderline Personality Disorder and consists in the tendency to view the world in black and white terms. Such an approach greatly undermines the possibility of healthy and stable personal interactions since it forces the Borderline person's emotions to cycle back and forth between two extremes. While undergoing feelings of intense highs (*Idealization*), the BPD individual will exaggerate positive qualities about themselves, about others, and about the world around them. On the other side of the coin are times of intense lows (*Devaluation*), in which they will focus on and exaggerate the negative aspects of these same objects. Within your own relationship, it is important to understand that your partner may very well be telling the truth about the positive elation they feel towards you today. This excitement is likely the real way that they feel about you in *this particular moment.* But these expressions coming from a Borderline person are merely a sign that they are in the midst of an Idealization phase, and there is no way of telling how long this phase will last. At the drop of a hat, they can undergo a rapid mood swing into a Devaluation phase, leading to a complete change in the way they feel about themselves, you, and the world in general. Let us get more specific with how this behavioral cycle develops.

The Initial Signs of Trouble

We have already explained that when you start dating a Borderline person, they tend to make you feel special and important. But over time, this intense initial obsession displayed towards you will pass through several gradual changes. You will begin to realize that something is off, even though you may have difficulty pinpointing where or what exactly the problem is. Here is what is likely happening: your partner still seems to express a great deal of interest in you, but only as *an idealized version of you that lives within their own head.* They will start to ignore the *real you* who exists as a genuine person out in the world, independent of their own whims and machinations. You are an individual with your own interests, your own needs, and your own feelings, and in any healthy relationship your partner will acknowledge and respect this fact. A Borderline partner, however, tends to only think of you in relation to themselves and their owns wishes, and thus has a great deal of difficulty in conceiving of you as an independent entity with your own needs and desires.

The realization of this fact constitutes a great destabilizing element for you. *Indeed, your Borderline partner's obsession with you has been a major factor in your own fascination with them since the beginning of your relationship!* But their adoration is directed towards an abstract idealization of you that they have constructed in their own mind. No wonder you are confused! You may not really want to admit it, but the truth is that your feelings, opinions, and suggestions only matter to your partner when they are focused on them, because this aligns with the false version of you that they nurture and encourage. You sense that their emotions perk-up when your attention is drawn to their life and their problems. In such moments, your partner will treat you tenderly because they badly crave your support and approval. You in turn will feel rewarded by their attention, by how close you two are during those occasions. In the back of your mind, however, you experience confusion and puzzlement. You like feeling special and unique for this person, but what your partner appreciates and expects from you does not align with your true nature. Day by day, they are learning how to exploit your compassion in an attempt to make you give up your own needs and become what they want you to be. Equipped with the right tools, you can avoid this trap. But without explicit knowledge of the many intricacies of navigating a relationship with a person suffering from Borderline Personality Disorder, you are in danger of falling victim.

People with BPD can be masterful at eliciting compassion from those close to them and usually have an uncanny ability to recognize those most likely to offer it. They will rarely thank you for an empathetic outpouring on their behalf. Instead, as we have just discussed, they will use this to further take advantage of you. In your relationship with a Borderline person, you will learn that their problems are the center of their existence. And because, to them, you exist as an idealized construct in their mind, those problems must also become the center of *your* entire existence. *The world is against them! Their back is aching! Their head hurts! They are so hungover! They probably have diabetes, or maybe even cancer! They woke up this morning with a cold, which clearly means that they are dying of COVID!* These imagined, or at least very exaggerated, ailments will continue to appear and disappear throughout your relationship. If you keep track of them, you will likely notice that they often emerge or taper off in sync with the waning and waxing of your attention. Such attitudes are your partner's way of begging you, "Don't leave me! I need you!"

Remember that across the board instability is a staple trait in the life of someone with Borderline Personality Disorder, and no exceptions are extended to their personal relationships. At any given moment, your partner may swing from being depressed, anxious, nervous, or insecure, to being totally distant and unconcerned with you – or anything else – except their own problems. In the blink of an eye, they may go from elation to agitation to mournful gloom. Observing such unpredictable mood swings can be like following the needle on a Richter-scale map near the site of an active volcano. You never know which flick of the needle will signify a Mount St. Helens level eruption. After an emotional outburst, your partner may realize that their actions were wrong and beg for your forgiveness. If you have allowed yourself to be sucked into this chaotic internal tempest of theirs, you will likely stick around to monitor the coming eruption. You will tell yourself that you can figure out how to stave off the next outburst. But this is futile. If the two of you remain entrenched in the same behavioral patterns, then *there will always be another explosion.* The cycle will repeat itself until that day in which you will finally learn to recognize and reject the emotional abuse that has been cast upon you.

You are like a lifeguard on an ocean beach, and your partner is like a drowning person crying out for help. You risk your own life and well-being to swim out and save them from a watery grave. Once out of the choppy water, you do all that is in your power to comfort them, wrap them in a warm blanket, and reassure them that everything is going to be fine. But as soon as you look away from them, they run back into the water and begin to cry for help all over again. No matter how many times you come to their rescue, they continue to repeat the same behavioral pattern and eventually will need you to save them again. This is what it is like to maintain a close relationship with someone suffering from Borderline Personality Disorder. No matter what you do, no matter how hard you try, your efforts will never be enough in your partner's eyes. No amount of physical, financial, or emotional help seems to make a long-term difference. You continue to pour your heart and soul into them, but you are left to watch helplessly as all your love and care spiral down the drain. You cling to the hope that your endeavors will eventually matter, and that your partner is capable of change. Surely, all the emotional effort you have put into this relationship cannot have all been for naught. Or could it?

Your lover's emotional rollercoaster has now firmly taken you on as a passenger. You long for those wonderful highs that seemed to define your relationship at first, but more and more, you find yourself spending time in the lowest places. In spite of all this, you desperately want to stay with your partner, and you look for rationalizations for your choice. You tell yourself that it is too late to give up now. The effort you have put in up to this point makes you want to stay on the ride until the end. Furthermore, it is difficult to give up the times of joy and elation that have been imprinted in your mind. Your sex life during these highs can lead to moments of absolute ecstasy, and you feel as if your partner has connected with you like no other person in the universe could possibly do. This level of intimacy and obsession fills you with a burning desire that can take your breath away. But remember: *when your ability to breathe is taken away for too long of a time, you end up suffocating.*

Philosophers throughout the ages have spent a great deal of time pondering the roots of suffering and the role that suffering plays in our lives. The Buddha taught that one's desires are at the root of all the suffering they experience. Riffing off this, a very productive way to relieve your emotional suffering is to control your desires – especially those toxic ones that lead to negative feelings on a regular basis. Life with your Borderline partner moves at an extremely high speed, and each bend in the road exerts a crushing amount of centrifugal force upon you. The euphoria you experience during the high times of this intense ride is what you have been trained to desperately desire and underlies the reason that you have entered such an unstable relationship in the first place. You are being led by your desires that, increasingly, can only be satisfied through powerful emotional connection. Unfortunately, such strong passions usually constitute a dangerous double-edged sword.

A Borderline person has a built-in, turbulent emotionality that rubs off on you in ever increasing amounts as time goes on. Remember that they are filled with an instinctive – whether conscious or unconscious – desire to influence and control. Although many of the moments you spend with your partner can be enthralling, your partner is being driven by a desire to conquer. Once you have accepted that riding this high-speed rollercoaster is your new normal, things really start to spiral out of control. You spend hours seeking the exuberance that you experienced at the beginning of the relationship, only to find that those highs are not what they once were. In addition to this, the lows in the relationship seem to get lower, and occur with increasing frequency. You begin to question whether this person is right for you, but you find it extremely difficult to walk away because they have been imprinted on your mind. You do not want to disappoint them or let them down. You tell yourself, *"If only I could change myself a just little bit. Then we'd both be happy."* Thinking this way is a clear sign that you have become ensnared in their toxic emotional vortex. At this point, both of you realize that you are virtually incapable of leaving the relationship. This once timid and vulnerable seeming person has finally conquered you.

9

Out of the Frying Pan, into the Fire

A relationship with a Borderline person is full of whiplash. The paradoxical mood swings that you see in your partner often leave you second guessing yourself. You look inward and ask whether you are doing something to contribute to the frequent changes of your partner's mental state. This self-blame you feel is common for someone in your situation. All too frequently, it is part of the game they have been playing with you. The full effects of the dysfunctional relationship are only evident once they have gained full control over you. Their nasty side has partially revealed itself before, but the most negative qualities were disguised and tempered. Now that you have given up your resistance and allowed the relationship to solidify into its present state, these negative qualities will come out in full force. To deal with your BPD partner appropriately, you must remember that to them, you are more of a figment living in their mind than an independently existing being. *The image of you they cherish is not real,* and you do yourself a great disservice in trying to conform to it.

"My girlfriend told me she doesn't like the way I walk. What the hell? She said my stride is too 'bouncy', whatever that means and now I'm very self-conscious about it. I've even started to watch myself walk in front of the mirror and I realize now that I do walk with more bounce than normal people tend to have. Do others notice this too, but just have never said anything to me before? Maybe I can consciously change my stride and walk like a normal person should – but then I'd be afraid that my stride would look forced and unnatural. I wouldn't even really care about the way I walk, except it seems to bother her so much that I really think I should try and change it. I just want her to love me!"

When you choose to live independently and refuse to conform to the falsified version of you that your partner has constructed, the relationship will receive an emotional jolt. Your lover's behavior towards you was once characterized by ecstatic highs with some uncomfortable lows mixed in. But in this new phase in which you have given them such a huge level of control, these highs will occur less and less frequently. You have increasingly given up on your own needs and wishes and have resigned yourself to play completely by their rules. Of course, there can – and likely will – be moments of passionate intimacy and emotional connection. But this is part of the control mechanism that has conquered you. Without this idealized reward which is dangled out in front of you like a horse being led by a carrot on a stick, their absolute control over you would be impossible. You may realize this and, at times, even make a halfhearted attempt to stand up for yourself. But when your Borderline lover sees this, they have at their disposal a powerful strategy meant to set their hooks even deeper in you. This is the cycle of Passionate Rage and Passive Aggressive Dissociation.

Passionate Rage: Unprovoked Eruptions

It is puzzling and disturbing to watch an unprovoked display of rage show itself for the first time. The trigger that sets off such an episode is usually hard (if not impossible) to spot by an external observer. But these types of outbursts are completely warranted in the mind of the Borderline person. Their emotional flare-ups are justified in their eyes, and you, as their partner, are often the catalyst for them. They will blame you for purposely trying to hurt them, whether it is the sound of your voice, how you think, how you feel, how you dress, walk, breathe, or even the way you look at them. Such rage episodes are often spontaneous and can even culminate in physical violence. They are part of a deeper strategy aimed at eventually wearing you down and breaking you. Your self-esteem will plummet. In an effort to stop these episodes, you will question your actions and try to modify your behavior. Even though this might temporarily quell the storm, you can rest assured that it will eventually return with a vengeance.

"My wife tells me she loves it when I cook for her, and I regrettably don't do it as often as I should. Her birthday was last week, and I planned a wonderful meal that we could enjoy together. While she was away, I spent several hours preparing everything for dinner, thinking that this would really make her happy. But when she got home, she started yelling at me! 'What, are you embarrassed to go out with me in public? Why wouldn't you want to take me to my favorite restaurant? Do you not want to spend money on me? Why are you such a cheapskate?' She threw a pan of boiling noodles across the room and nearly burned me. She left the house in a rage and didn't answer her phone until several hours later. When we talked, she

admitted that she probably overreacted, but also said that I should have known what she wanted. I ended up apologizing and she came back home. We drank a bottle of wine and passionately made love. I'd do anything for this woman. What can I do to stop her from detesting me and all that I do?"

Caring for someone with Borderline Personality Disorder can quickly change from an experience of love and adoration to one of violence and abandonment. Negative outbursts aimed at you can cause intense psychic pain and will often lead you into a state of depression. Your partner's behavior distorts your perceptions, and the more puzzled and confused you get, the more aggressive and desperate they become. They realize that their conduct might have serious consequences, of which they are terrified. Their ensuing anguish and fear of being abandoned can lead your partner to commit self-harm and maybe even to threaten suicide. If you find yourself in this situation, proceed with caution as sometimes such desperate and hopeless feelings can extend to you. While Borderline Personality Disorder is a psychological condition that is not contagious in the sense of a physical disease, many of the negative feelings that your lover experiences can start to rub off and take root in you.

Here is an important realization that you must have: your Borderline lover is not the only one who is stuck in a loop of *idealization and devaluation.* You are doing this too, and their episodes of passionate rage rope you further into this cycle. You idealize a version of your partner that you have made up in your mind, one in which their positive qualities are emphasized, and the negative ones are ignored. At the same time, you devalue yourself after every one of their outbursts. Looking inward, you only see the negative aspects of your personality that your partner – and now also you – consider to be the cause of their rapid mood swings. At this point, you need to seek help. You have now come to accept your partner's distorted points of view, and your only hope to make things right is to seek the advice of an impartial voice of sanity.

Nothing in the real world is truly black or white. Everything occurs in various shades of gray, and your perception of a particular shade is heavily affected by both internal and external factors. When you start to see things in absolute terms like your Borderline lover does, you further entrench yourself in the patterns of an unhealthy and codependent relationship. Indeed, only looking at things in their absolute extremes goes hand-in-hand with the sort of Jekyll-and-Hyde personality duality that you see in your partner. Their abrupt mood swings can occur at any time, fluctuating drastically between an idealized and a devalued view of the world. You never know what to expect – what side of your lover will be shown to you the next time you see them. You spend your moments walking on eggshells, afraid to step out of line and cause another angry episode. But these efforts are futile. Your partner does not need your permission to flare up, and even the most innocuous little detail can become the pretext for the next eruption.

Passive Aggressive Dissociation: Silent Treatment

We have just seen how rage can be strategically used by Borderline people to consolidate power within their relationships. Another common way in which they exercise control over their partners is through an extreme form of passive aggressive behavior: the sudden refusal to acknowledge or respond to them. This is colloquially referred to as giving someone the *silent treatment.* Why do BPD sufferers sometimes express their anger by refusing to speak? Because they know that silence can be deafening. If you are in a relationship with a Borderline person, you likely have experienced how abusive this type of behavior can be. You are left to second guess yourself as to what you may have done to deserve this treatment. You rack your brain, desperately searching for an answer and trying to understand the way in which you stepped out of line. "Did I fold his pair of pants the wrong way? Am I using too much salad dressing? Did he misinterpret the compliment I gave him as an attack?" You are kept in the dark and have no idea how to remedy the situation. As with an unprovoked rage outburst, this method of control is particularly effective because it makes you question and doubt yourself; it forces you to look inward for a rational answer. The truth is that there rarely is a rational explanation for why you are receiving the silent treatment, the same way that there is no reason for their rage outbursts. Yet while the causes may be obscure, the effects are clear: silence gives the Borderline person a feeling of dominance which they can use as a mask for their own weaknesses.

"I was in the car with my boyfriend, returning from an amazing out-of-town weekend together. At a certain point I asked him if we could play some music on the radio. He started some jazz, which admittedly is not my favorite, but I was actually enjoying that particular song. He then said abruptly, 'You hate this, don't you?' I told him that this was not the case and that I liked the song. He immediately got angry, saying 'You are lying! Why can't you admit that you detest

this music? You always lie to me!' I tried to justify myself, but there was no way to convince him that I was being sincere. All of a sudden, he got silent and refused to talk to me for the rest of the ride home. He wouldn't even look at me. When we got to my house, he kept the car running and never got out to say goodbye. I took my suitcase out of the trunk and was left in tears on the side of the road while watching him speed away. What did I do wrong? This happened yesterday, and he still hasn't replied to my texts or returned my calls. How can I make him talk to me again?"

The silent treatment can be tactfully used in tandem with violent outbursts of rage. Such behaviors help Borderline people regulate their distance from their partner. In every relationship there should be a healthy balance on the amount of time the couple spends together. How often should you call or text each other throughout the day? If you are not living in the same house, how many nights a week should you spend together? And so on. But it is impossible to maintain a stable balance in the relationship with a BPD partner. A Borderline person is very inconsistent in the amount of attention they require. Sometimes they want you at arm's length, other times they reject you. You find yourself the object of a constant push and pull, the dynamics of which make the BPD person feel at ease and in control, able to continually make up their own rules. Flattery and over-the-top displays of affection pull you close, while red-hot rage and ice-cold silence are used to push you away.

When you are given the silent treatment, two simultaneous things happen. On the one hand you feel weak, helpless, and confused. You wonder if maybe you did something to deserve this. On the other hand, you begin to try and rationalize your partner's behavior, telling yourself that the silent treatment is in some ways preferable to a volcanic outburst. Silence starts to look to you as the better alternative in a dysfunctional dichotomy. This way of looking at things is flat out wrong. Both options are bad, and you should not prefer one to the other. By allowing yourself to think your partner's use of the weaponized silence is justified in any way – "At least I'm not being yelled at" – you are agreeing to live by their rules. You have given them control and renounced your right to be treated with respect.

Remember that a Borderline person feels entitled in having their own needs met, and that they neither realize nor care how these demands affect you. If you attempt to resist your partner's wishes, they will often escalate the situation and become even more demanding. But then at other times, they might temporarily drop the issue and will abruptly refuse to even acknowledge your presence. The silent treatment is such a powerful tool to the Borderline person because it allows for the unimpeded growth of seeds that have already taken root in your mind. Though your partner refuses to speak, their demands continue to ring loudly. You want them to come back and to interact with you again, thus making it much more likely for you to cave in to their demands. You want more than anything for the silence to end, and the longer it continues, the more you are willing to dance upon their puppet strings. Such behavior on your part then reinforces the effectiveness of their strategy, making it increasingly likely that they will use it over and over and over again.

Behavior Driven by Fear of Rejection

When a Borderline person is in an idealization phase, their exuberance lifts you like a raft on the ocean during high tide. You tell yourself that this is the time that they will stay like this. But you have been through this cycle too many times to actually believe such nonsense deep down. Just like the raft floating upon the sea, you know that as the Earth continues to turn, the tides will fall, and you'll be dashed violently upon rocks. Maybe this will be the time that will irrevocably break you into a million tiny pieces. Even as you lie there broken, your partner still blames you for their pain. They are vindictive, and seek to punish you with hurtful gestures, with silence, and with deception – all the while seeking to damage your self-image and deflate your self-esteem. This situation is in many ways akin to the ocean getting mad at the raft, scapegoating it as the reason it fell from its own high tide.

We have described in the first part of this book how people with BPD keep experiencing *dissociation* throughout their life: at times, they stop taking in input from the outside world and simply rely on their inner perceptions. Fixating upon the images that they have built in their mind amplifies both the magnitude and the negativity of their thoughts and emotions. Nowhere is this more apparent than in their immense trust issues. Borderline people are extremely suspicious of everyone's actions and words. *Such mistrust is not rooted in reality and is only based on their delusional inner world.* Because of the skewed perception of what is going on around them, they might become at times very insecure, constantly seeking advice, and asking repeatedly the same questions to many people (especially their partner): "Am I a worthwhile person? Am I worthy of being loved?" This needy and clingy behavior exhibited by a BPD sufferer is a natural response to their deep fears of abandonment, and is fueled – as we have seen – by their irrational skepticism. They want to be loved and cared for, but they do not trust anyone, and will obsessively look around them for signs of rejection. Small things such as being late or canceling an appointment for a legitimate reason are enough to send them into a tailspin. Trust is a constant problem for BPD sufferers, often leading them to levels of extreme paranoia.

"My boyfriend will angrily confront me whenever I leave my phone on silent or don't immediately respond to his texts. A few weeks ago, I saw his car out in the parking lot of the restaurant where I work. I was startled that he was in his car watching me through the window, and when I checked my phone, I was truly shocked! I had 27 text messages from him saying at first that he didn't believe I was working and that I was being unfaithful. In this chain of messages, he had started accusing me of flirting with my manager! This is just ridiculous! He doesn't believe me, and I feel so bad that he's worried that I'm sleeping around behind his back. What can I change to make him feel better? I really love him and don't know what I should do. He constantly tells me he's not good enough for me. He's even suggested that we'd both be better off if he was dead. Maybe it's me who isn't good enough for him! He can be so devoted and loving when we're together."

To your Borderline partner, you are either fully in their corner or fully against them. It is nearly impossible to defend yourself against accusations of disloyalty or to clarify a perceived injustice. If you try and justify yourself, they may purposefully escalate the situation, thus provoking your anger. This then gives them in turn an excuse to go off on you and reinforces their belief that their initial accusations were justified. Remember that, in their desperate quest for sympathy, Borderline people are capable of all sorts of emotional coercion and possibly even violence. And if you think that your status as a partner should have earned you a certain level of trust, you cannot be more wrong: in the eyes of BPD person, their partner, their friends, and their relatives are *the most likely* to betray them.

Gaslighting and Reality Distortion

The term *gaslighting* comes from the 1940s film Gaslight. Gregory, the main character, manipulates a woman's gas lights in her home so that they dim when she feels alone. His deceit causes her to believe she is dreaming the dimming, eventually leading her to doubt her sanity. Today, gaslighting is described as the intentional dissemination of false or distorted information with the intent of interfering with a person's ability to trust their senses, thoughts, and memory of events. People with Borderline Personality Disorder are often skilled gaslighters, at both a conscious and subconscious level. Why would someone do this? The misrepresentation of reality, the withholding of details, or outright retelling of events in an attempt to change the past is done so that you are no longer able trust your own reactions and memories. By making you feel nervous and insecure, they have a better chance of maneuvering you and sucking you into the confines of their inner world, where they feel safe, secure, and most importantly in control.

"My partner can be the most wonderful person much of the time, but he seems to exist inside his own reality distortion field. The problem is, his distorted perceptions rub off on me and make me question even the most basic things that I would usually take for granted. Last week we had a brutal argument where he broke things around the house and threatened to become violent. Then a few hours later, after we had apologized to each other for arguing, he flat out told me that I was the one who knocked over the bookshelf and shattered several picture frames we had there! I remember seeing him do this! But he can be so convincing when he tells me that I did this that I honestly start to second guess my memory. I get so scared and so upset when we argue in that way that I guess I could be imaging him breaking things. Did I black out and make up this memory? The truth is that I don't want to know the truth. I'm afraid that if I push the issue, he'll leave me. I guess I'd rather not know which one of us knocked over the bookshelf. This event is in the past, and I don't think it will do any good to continue to focus on it."

10

Assessing a Codependent Relationship

Since Borderline sufferers often lack the agency to carry out many basic societal functions, they tend to seek out partners who can assist them with their struggles and help them perform daily tasks. They also look for people who can provide stability and can help them keep their volatile emotions in check. Your BPD partner will seem to external observers to be the underdog in the relationship, while you probably give off the air of being the rational decision maker. Behind closed doors, however, the dynamics are usually reversed. *You are the underdog, and your partner decides the direction of your relationship – although in a way that can hardly be described as rational.* The two of you are codependent, but the way in which this manifests itself is significantly different in you than it is in your partner.

You spend your days living for the high moments of the relationship and stake your own well-being around your connection to your partner. Most importantly, you are also willing to change your behavior and lifestyle in order to accommodate your partner's wishes. But what does this codependent relationship look like from their point of view? Well, you are also the focal point of their existence – but as we have already discussed, the "you" we are talking about is just an idealized version of you that exists in your partner's mind. Their impulsive actions are a strategy to mold you into this false version of you that they have created. As long as you let your behavior be controlled and determined by their outbursts, silences, and mood swings, this unhealthy cycle of chaos and imbalance will continue. You have become their emotional caregiver – often to the point of self-neglect – and *as you hand over more and more authority to your partner, you further cement the dynamics of this unhealthy relationship*. Allowing your Borderline partner to take charge of the relationship sets it on a path toward ultimate destruction.

Living such a codependent relationship is like walking across a river on a rotted-out bridge. Some of your steps may seem solid and stable, but you know that you could fall through at any moment. You are never sure what consequences your next step will have, which leaves you disoriented and insecure. So, what can you do? Is the relationship inevitably doomed? Absolutely… *unless* you take charge of the situation. First and foremost, *you must do what is right for you*! Setting limits within your relationship may or may not help your partner come to terms with their irrational thinking, but it is an absolute necessity for your own well-being. It is a good idea to call their bluff in a levelheaded and non-threatening way. You need to build your own self-esteem and learn to be more assertive. Taking positive steps to emotionally repair yourself is the only way that this relationship can possibly improve, but you should not use the relationship as the primary motivation driving your actions. *You owe it to yourself to make these changes.* As long as your relationship remains entrenched in its present state of codependence, the quality of your life will continue to decline. *You need to make yourself and your own well-being the main focal point of the next phase in your life.*

Taking Positive Steps to Heal Yourself

Where do you go from here? People who are confident and comfortable with themselves understand the difference between reasonable and outrageous behavior, and are therefore able to make sensible and informed choices. They can also stand by their decisions and act accordingly. In contrast to this, being in an unhealthy relationship with a Borderline partner can cloud one's judgement due to repeated manipulation and gaslighting. Moreover, it is likely that your partner has worked hard to separate you from friends, family, and other sources of support. This is part of a well-developed strategy to make you feel less confident and comfortable, and therefore less likely to abandon them. Whether they are doing this consciously or unconsciously, the end outcome is the same. Social isolation is a gradual process that does not happen overnight, and you may only realize it after months or even years. It can be shocking to become aware of just how much this toxic relationship has corroded your social support network, leaving you disconnected and alone. You need to act with urgency if you are to change this situation.

Before you decide on any course of action, you need to make an honest assessment of your relationship. The number one thing you should do is to seek information and advice on how to deal with a Borderline partner. That is the reason this book was written.

Ask yourself the following questions:

- Do you avoid social situations because your partner's conduct is so embarrassing?
- Do you have a fear of telling your friends and family the truth about your relationship?
- When you leave the house for a few hours, does your partner question you about where you are going, how long you will be gone, and who you will be seeing? Do they sometimes make unreasonable accusations?
- Do you feel as if your partner is overly obsessed with you at some moments and completely detached at others?
- Does your partner spend time putting your friends and family down as a way to overshadow their own failures?
- Is your partner continually interfering with your plans to socialize with others?
- Has your partner given you a false retelling of events after one of your fights to try to gaslight you into questioning your own reality?
- Do you often find yourself anticipating your partner's reaction before you make a decision?

If you answered yes to any of these questions, then you are in need of outside advice. In the next chapter, several courses of action are outlined, some that involve repairing the relationship and others that involve ending it. The path you choose is a crucial decision, and one you must make by putting yourself and your own well-being above anything else.

IV

MANAGING THE RELATIONSHIP

11

Improving the Relationship

In the last chapters, we have described many common traits you may experience throughout the course of your relationship with a Borderline partner. We ended the most recent chapter with a list of questions to help you assess your situation. If the answer to any of those questions was yes, you must decide on the course of action that you plan to take. In what follows, we suggest strategies to better manage the circumstances you face. But before we do, *we must make it absolutely clear that you should never put up with an abusive situation.* The unpleasant episodes you may experience in your relationship are never something that you deserve, nor are they ever something that you should make excuses for. You should only stay with your partner if you believe that the unhealthy aspects of the relationship can be addressed and properly dealt with.

The strategies outlined below are designed to lead to noticeable improvements in *your* life. Whether you like it or not, you must realize that your partner's behavior is ultimately out of your control. How they choose to deal with their condition is up to them, and them alone. You can – and should – be supportive and encouraging, but can never force them to change. They must both desire and work toward these changes themselves. If they are not willing to make a serious commitment to overcoming their personality disorder, then you will have no choice but to leave. But if they are ready to recognize their issues and agree to deal with them properly, your relationship can be nursed back to a loving and healthy one.

Managing Your Partner's Outbursts

When you are in a relationship with someone suffering from BPD, you will often have to endure episodes of anger and rage. What is the best way to react under such circumstances? It is natural to feel like you should treat your partner in the way they have treated you. *Have they caused you pain?* Then you may have the urge to hurt them back. *Have they made you feel sad, insecure, or scared?* Then there are times when you probably wanted to retaliate. But despite such impulses, fighting fire with fire will only lead to additional chaos and never to the healing that you long for. You must ask yourself: *What am I trying to achieve here?* An eye for an eye will leave the whole world blind.

Giving in to your own angry impulses in order to get even with your partner adds fuel to an already volatile blaze. A fire that may have been easily contained at an early stage becomes a dangerous inferno after dousing it with gasoline. Keep things in perspective and remember that your angry feelings will not last forever. Wait patiently and let your partner calm down. If you choose to escalate the situation, their foul mood and behavior will only grow worse. Heated exchanges almost always end with both parties saying hurtful things with lasting negative consequences and leaving scars that are difficult to heal.

Here is an extremely important point: *You are not responsible for your partner's erratic behavior!* Nothing that you did or said merited their actions, regardless of what they may tell you. You did not do anything to deserve abusive criticism. Your partner's anger is a symptom of their Borderline personality – an expression of the violent struggles that they are experiencing inside. As you listen closely to their rage-filled screams, you will come to realize that they are less like a dangerous animal and more like a helpless child.

You can try to calmly talk to your partner in an attempt to de-escalate the situation, but proceed with caution. In such heated moments, logical reasoning tends not to resonate. Your partner is acting on emotion and is incapable of listening to rational arguments. It is not the right moment to engage in detailed explanations or to put forward demands, even if they are quite reasonable and you show your best goodwill in presenting them. You might be tempted to make your partner promise that such a situation will never happen again. *"You have to swear this is the last time!"* While this seems like a valid demand to make, it will likely leave them feeling cornered and further exacerbate their fight-or-flight instincts. They will feel inadequate and ashamed that they were unable to control their temper, likely re-igniting fears of abandonment. Afraid that this may be the last time you are willing to put up with such behavior, they will become desperate and dig themselves into an even deeper hole.

Approaching your partner with zero-tolerance demands during one of their outbursts will only cut off communication. If the goal is to engage with them in a meaningful dialogue, you must be flexible. You should ask what is troubling them, and then be willing to listen. Be prepared to endure long moments of silence. Let them speak first and try not to get defensive. They may be waiting for you to say something that they can disagree with, establishing a new pretext for tension, a spark to reignite the fight. Do not fall into this trap. Use few words, ask open-ended questions, and wait patiently for their answers.

Here is another thing to keep in mind: *Do not focus on trying to change your partner.* You will never achieve this goal by your own will alone. You can, however, act as a positive influence. Strive to create an environment that fosters cooperation rather than control. Make sure they understand that you are an ally and not an enemy – that you are aware of their distress and suffering – and that you are willing to support them as they take the first steps to address their condition.

Sometimes sitting down to talk is not the best strategy. Perhaps meaningful communication is impossible at that moment. Or maybe you just cannot stand being yelled at any longer. In such circumstances, it is okay to take a break. Calmly say that you are going for a walk and that you will talk later. If such a fight takes place over the phone, you can propose to resume the discussion in person. Taking a temporary pause from confrontation often serves to cool tempers. Just make sure you both realize that these problems will not go away on their own and must be dealt with eventually.

Your partner's outbursts are cries for help, even if they never admit it. It might seem that they want to keep you around simply as a punching bag, but it is often more complicated than that. Temporarily walking away from them could cause them to take a step back and reconsider their behavior. This will yield positive results, with your partner eventually reaching out to you and perhaps even apologizing. But outright ignoring them and giving them the cold shoulder will increase their fears of abandonment, making it more likely that you will pay a high price for this perceived desertion. There needs to be at least one adult in the room here. Engaging in childish and immature games is never appropriate. Learn to trust your judgement and stick to your guns when making decisions.

A Borderline personality is characterized by extremely inconsistent behavior, and this inconsistency extends to reactions to your actions. The same words might produce different outcomes on different days. It is up to your own judgement to decide when it is better to attempt communication and when it is better just to walk away.

While there is no one-size-fits-all recipe to tell you how to respond in these situations, there are several general rules to be inferred from the discussion above.

First, a summary of behaviors in which you should not engage:

- Do not get angry.
- Do not humiliate your partner.
- Do not seek revenge.

- Do not call your partner names. (*"You're crazy!"*)
- Do not take their actions personally.
- Do not act in a way that would make them feel inadequate.
- Do not present them with unrealistic demands.
- Do not try to force a change in them.

Now a list of recommended behaviors:

- Be aware at all times of your partner's suffering.
- De-escalate the situation.
- Wait for their anger to subside.
- Maintain your composure.
- Give them a possibility of backtracking.
- Create a positive environment to foster communication.
- Try to be helpful and supportive.
- Ask open-ended questions.
- Be patient and accept long intervals of silence.
- Know if/when to walk away.

Managing Your Partner's Self-Abuse

People suffering from Borderline Personality Disorder struggle to cope when things are not going the way they want or expect. They will frequently blame themselves for their failures, and as a result they may carry out acts of self-punishment. During a relationship with a Borderline person, you may witness episodes of self-harm. These can take many different forms: both in overt and shocking displays such as cutting, burning or threats of suicide, and in other sorts of self-destructive behaviors such as chain smoking, binge eating, excessive drinking, or drug abuse. There are also other types of harmful behaviors that may not pose a risk to their physical well-being but can nonetheless have dire consequences for their future. For example, they may threaten to quit their job, to move to another country, or even to leave their spouse and children. Again, as with their outbursts of anger, *these are cries for help*. It is best to operate under the working assumption that they will carry out their threats if they do not find emotional relief.

It can be very painful to see your partner engage in self-destructive acts. When you witness this in someone you care about, you may feel guilty, confused, angry, or frustrated. But you must recognize your own limitations. You are not to blame for your partner's behaviors. This point was made in the previous section, and the same discussion applies again here. Do not lose your temper with them, and do not start a debate. Your partner cannot be won over with logic and reasoning while engaged in self-destructive behaviors any more than they can during an angry outburst aimed at you.

Here are some more general rules that can be added to the lists of the previous section.

What you should NOT do while witnessing an episode of self-harm:

- Do not label self-harm as "attention seeking". While there may be truth to this at some level, it is not what your partner needs to hear in such moments. Making this accusation is counter-productive and will only trigger embarrassment and insecurity.
- While you should not completely ignore their self-inflicted

injuries, you also should not overly focus on them. Remember that self-harm is a way for your Borderline partner to project their suffering to the outside world, to make it concrete. By over focusing on their acts of self-harm, you may give them the impression that you only understand their pain when their scars are visible.

- Do not try to find a logical motivation underlying their actions. Remember that oftentimes they themselves are not aware of the root causes behind these behaviors.
- Avoid the use of physical restraint unless absolutely necessary. Doing this will put them into fight-or-flight mode, dangerously escalating the situation. If they are binge eating or chain smoking, do not confiscate their food or cigarettes. More generally, do not act or communicate in any way that they might perceive to be an attempt to seize control away from them.
- Do not blame yourself. Whatever happens, you are not accountable for your partner's actions and behaviors.

Here are some guidelines on what to do instead:

- If, at any time, you fear for your own or for your partner's physical safety, call the police or a healthcare professional immediately.
- Reach out to your partner's therapist in the case that they already have one.
- Act in a way that will let them feel in control of their decisions.
- Calmly remind them of any alternative coping mechanisms that might have worked during previous episodes of this kind.

- Try to establish a conversation with your partner while maintaining a positive and non-judgmental attitude. Remind them of their good qualities and of things they do well. Try to have them talk about past successes and accomplishments. Focus on activities and experiences that made them happy and could help beat back their pervading sense of emptiness.
- If your partner's self-destructive behavior does not seem to be life-threatening, you can politely tell them that you are going to leave for a while. As is the case in outbursts aimed at you, this strategy may cause them to reconsider their conduct.

Managing Abuse Directed towards You

The only way to deal with a truly abusive situation is to walk away from it. Unfortunately, this is easier said than done. There are many factors that can prevent you from leaving such a relationship. Some are linked to material circumstances, such as the presence of children or a lack of financial independence. But there are also psychological barriers preventing you from taking this step. *To break free, you will need to focus on yourself and abandon any deeply ingrained, delusional beliefs about the relationship.*

People with Borderline Personality Disorder usually do not set out to hurt their partners. Instead, they respond to their own fears and insecurities with outbursts of emotion, lashing out in what they perceive to be self-defense. But in the end, it does not matter what their motives are because the consequences on you are the same. Violence is never appropriate, whether your partner intends to be malicious or not. This applies to all forms of violence, whether physical or psychological. It is important to point out that relationships are rarely abusive from the beginning and are known to progressively worsen over time.

Even when one is fully aware of ongoing abuse, it can be difficult to walk away. The question now arises as to when such altercations with your partner qualify as abuse. Any of the negative traits of a relationship with a Borderline person discussed earlier in the book (shaming, gaslighting, making excessive demands, giving the silent treatment, etc.) could potentially merit the label "abuse". If you are experiencing these types of behaviors in your relationship, you need to tell others about it. Talk to a close friend or family member. Hearing the opinion of a person on the outside can help you identify escalating signs of abuse. If you are still unsure after consulting with friends or family, you should seek the advice of a therapist. Trained professionals can provide a level-headed assessment of your situation and guide you along your next steps.

Another valuable strategy is to keep a personal journal of your experiences. This is an excellent way to organize the details of your relationship, both in the present and for the future. It will help you make sense of the day-to-day goings on with your partner, in addition to preserving a record of events for a later time in case you ever choose to confront them. We have seen how Borderline people can gaslight you into feeling irrational, clouding both your memory and understanding. This makes it absolutely essential to keep a record of your experiences. You should write down everything that was said and done, paying close attention to the details. Looking back on your journal entries, you will be able to accurately track the level of abuse that you have allowed yourself be subjected to.

You should be always alert and watch out for abusive behavior. What should you do during an episode of violent abuse? If you are worried for your physical safety, the best thing you can do is to take your children, a few essential documents, and get out of there as soon as possible. Do not threaten to leave; just leave, and then call the police.

In the case that you do not feel physically threatened, you can try to de-escalate the confrontation by using the strategies we suggested at the beginning of this chapter.

Here is a summary of the relevant points:

- Take control of your own emotions; giving in to them will just exacerbate the situation.
- Do not try to argue or disagree with your partner. If you do chat, keep it short and sweet. Do not say anything that they will be able to use against you.
- Do not fight back, but at the same time never concede that any of their abuse is justified.
- Take no responsibility for your partner's actions. Abusive conduct is unacceptable, even if they claim that you deserve it.
- Do not threaten to leave them for good, even if this is what you ultimately decide to do.
- Agree to meet and discuss things later after everyone has calmed down.

- Do not accept apologies until verbal harassment has stopped.
- Once the situation has cooled off, tell your partner how much the incident affected you and how you would like to support them in seeking help to address their condition.

We end this chapter by repeating our fundamental message. These strategies outlined here will help you mitigate the negative impact that an abusive relationship has on you. But if the abuse persists, there is no choice but to walk away. The next chapter will tell you what to expect from a breakup and how to handle it in a healthy and balanced way.

12

Ending the Relationship

Given the inherent instability found in relationships where one of the two suffers from Borderline Personality Disorder, the non-Borderline partner will often entertain thoughts of ending the relationship. They find themselves stuck in a perpetual state of oscillation, cycling between love and hate in parallel with their Borderline partner's indecisive moods and feelings.

"Each night I find myself asking 'Am I doing the right thing in keeping this relationship alive? Should I give him another chance?' I feel so frustrated, but at the same time I am not resolute enough to walk away. Why is he behaving like this towards me? I really hate him in these moments. I have the urge to slap him in the hope of bringing him to his senses. Sometimes I really want to hurt him; I just hate him for how badly he makes me feel about myself. But I also love him. I wish I had never met him; I wish he didn't exist."

Any breakup can be difficult, but breaking up with someone with BPD is usually more complicated, and can be quite disturbing and painful. Oftentimes, partners of Borderline people will say that it is simply impossible for them to end the relationship. It is like quitting a bad habit that has become addictive, like smoking, drinking, gambling, or doing drugs. There will always be withdrawal symptoms, and oftentimes relapses, making it difficult to sustain your will and go forward with the breakup. In this codependent relationship that you find yourself in, it is difficult to stay away from your partner for a short period of time, let alone remove them from your life permanently.

Should I Stay or Should I Go?

Deciding whether or not you should continue in the relationship with your Borderline partner can be one of the most difficult decisions you will ever make. Even though you may have endured excessive abuse and trauma, your partner can still be charming, compassionate and caring at times. They may sense that you are contemplating a breakup and will try to pre-empt this by ramping up affection toward you. It is common to experience painful guilt when you think of leaving your partner, an issue that is greatly compounded whenever children are involved.

"I think about breaking up with her so often. But then I remember how much I love her. Besides, what will she do without me? She is so unstable, and I seem to be the only one who understands her suffering. She might hurt herself if I leave her. She might even – God forbid – commit suicide. Is it even morally right for me to walk away? I feel like I would be letting her down. I love her so much that I am ready to sacrifice my happiness to help her."

Can the relationship ever be healthy and satisfying if you are not pursuing your own happiness in it? Let us be clear. We are not recommending that you simply abandon your partner. If no actual violence is being perpetrated against someone in the household, if the Borderline individual recognizes their problem and commits to pursuing treatment, and if some signs of progress appear over time, then staying in the relationship remains a possibility.

Try to answer the following questions honestly.

- How long have you experienced ups and downs in dealing with your partner? When was the last time you were truly happy, when you felt stable, respected, and safe in your relationship?
- How many times has a discussion degenerated into verbal abuse, or into physical or psychological violence? How many such episodes have you experienced? Have they left deep scars in you?
- How many times have you already told yourself that things will change? Has anything actually changed?
- Have you given up hope that things can be different?
- Do you often think about the happy times at the beginning of the relationship, desperately wishing that they would come back?
- Do you have to constantly repeat to yourself that your partner really cares about you? Do you cling to some specific episodes to reassure yourself about your partner's feelings?
- Are you staying in the relationship because you are excited about it? Because you really cherish and enjoy the moments

that you and your partner spend together? Or is it more because you are worried about leaving?

- Is what you are experiencing true love or is it an unhealthy emotional dependence?
- How much is "saving your partner" a factor in you staying in the relationship? How much are you affected by the fact that you care about them, and you think they will not do well without you?

Contemplating these questions will help you make your choice. Even when an answer is clear in the depths of your mind, it is better to hear yourself ask the question out loud. Open up about the issues in your relationship. Talk to a therapist, or at least to a family member or close friend. Even if they do not offer a single point of advice, you will find it useful. Saying things out loud will let the reality of your situation sink in, and perhaps also help you regain the belief that you have a right to be happy.

Leaving an Abusive Relationship

If you plan to leave an abusive relationship, one in which you have experienced violence, you should follow these guidelines:

- Do not tell your partner that you are leaving.
- Consult your therapist or attorney for information on local services such as domestic abuse shelters.
- Make a bag with copies of important documents such as account numbers, birth certificates, health records, education records, insurance plans, your marriage license, along with a collection of car and house keys.

- Fill a suitcase with some changes of clothing for you and your kids.
- Place these items in a location where your partner will not be able to find them, such as a friend or neighbor's home.
- Withdraw some money and store it safely.
- Consider devising a code word for your children and friends to use when they need to summon assistance for you.
- Abstain from using drugs or alcohol during this time. This situation is difficult enough to navigate when sober.
- Leave a note for your partner describing how to reach you through your lawyer.
- Do not have one last altercation. When your partner is out of the house and unlikely to return until after your departure, simply go.

Some of these suggestions might come across as harsh or excessively punitive. However, if there has been a history of violence in your relationship, failing to take these precautions could jeopardize your safety. Moreover, it is vital to protect and shelter your children from any form of violent conflict.

Leaving a Non-Abusive Relationship

Not every relationship with a Borderline person is abusive. Nonetheless, after a careful evaluation of your situation, you might still decide that it is best to put an end to it. If you find yourself in this position, consider taking the following steps:

- Plan ahead of time. Before speaking with your partner, consult with an attorney about legal issues.

- Make no more attempts at reconciliation when you are confident of your decision.
- Maintain your composure. Deliver the message succinctly, and do not repeat yourself. Your partner does not need a lengthy clarification. Keep your speech short, pleasant, and to the point.
- Try to avoid further interaction after leaving. (A more thorough discussion on how to maintain no contact with your former partner will be presented in the next chapter). Be aware that this issue can be greatly complicated when it comes to children and joint custody.
- When you tell your partner about your decision, do not be deterred by their attempts to change your mind.
- After you have had your chat with your partner, follow through by leaving as soon as possible. Even if there has not been any past violence, remaining in their company can become dangerous. If things go worse than you expected, consider having a few friends or relatives available as an emergency backup.
- Expect your Borderline partner to be troubled and distressed by the news that you are leaving. This is the result of their fears of abandonment. It is not your fault, and there is nothing you can do about it. You might be bombarded with e-mails, text messages, pleading phone calls, stalking, or even suicide threats. If you need psychological assistance with these problems, speak to a therapist. You might also need to call the police if your ex-partner starts behaving in a particularly threatening manner.

After you have followed through with your breakup plans, you may have moments when you feel terrible. *You must realize that you are not mourning the relationship that you were living but only what it could have been, or what it should have been.* The next chapter will help you deal with the consequences of the breakup.

13

How to Endure a Breakup

It can be extremely hard to let go of your codependent relationship. Even if you rationally understand that leaving is the best course of action, the emotional bond with your partner can make you feel as if you are giving up a part of yourself. Why is it so difficult to cope with this breakup? Why is it far more challenging and painful than other breakups that you have experienced in the past? Is it because your partner was one-of-a-kind? Certainly, they are unique, like every individual is. However, you need to understand that the depth of this grief is due more to the complexities of your relationship than specifically to the person you are leaving behind. Your life has changed significantly because of all this. You have put in a tremendous amount of effort trying to make it work, and you might have even made important life choices based on what you perceived to be the best interest for the two of you as a couple. Your partner and their issues have therefore become parts of you. You have felt an immense amount of motivation to help resolve their problems. At some point, this effort gave your days meaning, making you feel both noble and valued. To achieve the ambitious goal of saving your partner and making the relationship work, you were willing to put up with habits that you previously found intolerable. But you remained adamant about seeing it done, no matter how hard it was. You cherished the feeling that your Borderline companion was yours to take care of and that you would never be separated.

Now that the relationship is over, you are probably overwhelmed with thoughts about what your former partner is doing, how they are coping, whether they are thinking about you, or if they are already seeing someone else. You constantly wonder if they ever really loved you and find yourself fixating on the question of why things had to end. You are enveloped in pain, disbelief, and frustration. It is important for you to remember that your Borderline partner was already on a challenging journey even before the relationship began. You were their knight in shining armor, a ray of light, an antidote to the disappointments that had bothered them for much of their lives. After the break-up, you can have pity on your former partner, but it has to stop there. You are doing what is best for you, and that is the bottom line.

Ten False Beliefs You Should Get Rid of

Your suffering is rooted in certain misconceptions which need to be addressed if you want to overcome your pain and move on with your life.

False Belief #1: The trust in your partner's abilities to make you happy.

You probably believe that your Borderline partner is in charge of your pleasure and your suffering. They are the person that can hurt you the most, but also the one who can make you feel whole again. They are the source of your joy as well as your pain. This belief has likely been present throughout most of your relationship, since much of your time was spent thinking and worrying about them.

As hard as it can be to accept right now, this perspective is entirely false. *The supposed ability of your partner to make you happy and complete was part of your own idealization process.* Remember that both you and your Borderline lover were caught in a cycle of idealization and devaluation. Even the attention you received from them was in response to their idealization of you. It was a courting ritual, not something based on true and stable feelings – no matter how genuine they may have felt at that specific time. You must also realize that a lot of the "happiness" you experienced with your partner came, not from what you were living, but from your expectations and dreams about the future, from an unrealistic conviction that this temporary elation could be made to last. Such thoughts were delusional but constituted an integral part of the idealization process. If you have recently ended an intense and traumatic relationship, you will likely be frustrated and unable to assess the situation rationally. But you owe it to yourself to be honest and realistic. Stop relying on your ex-partner as a source of fake happiness. Once you are able to give up on this false belief, it will cease to be a cause of pain.

False Belief #2: The belief that your ex-partner is having the same thoughts as you.

If you believe your ex-partner is going through the breakup in the same way you are, do not hold your breath. This will only add to your confusion and make it much more challenging to move on. Your relationship has ended because the two of you were on different pages. Communication often was not honest, and for the most part, you never truly understood each other. There is no reason to think that you have finally broken through barriers to achieve a true understanding now. Stop thinking about your ex-partner and trying to guess how they feel. While it is good to be compassionate, it is impossible to fully understand a Borderline person's thought process.

False Belief #3: Your conviction that the relationship's challenges were your fault.

Do you really believe your ex-partner to be credible and reliable in their analysis of the relationship? Borderline people have an uncanny ability to exploit insecurities and twist reality. This is a complex defensive mechanism – a denial mode – and a typical symptom of Borderline Personality Disorder. As a result of their gaslighting, you may have come to share your ex-partner's belief that you were the obstacle standing in the way of relationship success. You might feel like you are incomplete and need to change yourself, and that if you do not, you deserve to be punished or discarded. This is the reason why you accepted their punitive habits, and why you now feel guilty for letting them down.

This is nonsense. While there are always things that we can work on to fix ourselves, it takes two to tango. More than likely, your ex-partner's personality disorder played an outsized role in the disintegration of your relationship. You could spend eternity going through past events with a fine-toothed comb, continually finding little things that you might have done differently. But doing this would be akin to ignoring a vast forest for a few small trees. Your partner's inability to see reality and face their problems was the leading factor in your breakup.

False Belief #4: The belief in the triumphant force of love.

In economics they say that there is no such thing as a free lunch. The same is true in love: no relationship comes for free, not even when authentic love is present in the couple. A positive initial input from both parties is always needed. To be able to give that input, both people must be stable and grounded in reality. This was never the case throughout your toxic and codependent relationship. Both you and your ex-partner have a lot of work to do on your own personalities before any of these dysfunctional dynamics can be corrected. Feelings and affection alone can never overcome more serious issues in a relationship.

False Belief #5: The wish that things could return to a past that never actually existed.

When you are physically distant from your ex-partner, it is possible that you will start to forget the bad moments – their angry outbursts and your frequent disagreements, along with the abuse and violence that may have been present during your time together. If you are not careful, this forgetfulness can usher in a new idealization process on your part. Keep in mind that idealization is a symptom of a fragile and unhealthy situation, not one rooted in reality. Now that your partner is no longer with you, your memories might start to play tricks and create a past of happiness that never actually existed.

False Belief #6: Holding on to unfulfilled promises.

Be careful not to cling to your ex-partner's whispered promises and positive words while ignoring or downplaying their negative behaviors. These words must be discarded, even if it is hard for you to do so. The concrete actions you experienced during your tumultuous relationship speak several orders of magnitude louder than empty words ever could.

False Belief #7: The thought that if you had spoken loudly enough, your words would have been heard.

Perhaps you still believe that if you had articulated things more clearly, written them down, said them louder, or simply used better phrasing, then maybe you would have been understood. Perhaps you wish you had one last chance to talk to your ex-partner. This time you would prepare a more unambiguous and effective speech to convey your concerns and feelings. This is all for nothing. *The things you said were heard, comprehended, and ignored.* Look back upon your entire relationship. How many times did you ask the same questions, express the same worries, or repeat the same requests? It would be useless to try another time.

The more you pursue this strategy, the more you will be viewed as vulnerable, clingy, and pathetic. Forcing new communication will place you into another uncomfortable situation that will only lead to further frustration. You have already experienced that feeling of talking to a wall. You need to stop beating yourself up and simply let go.

False Belief #8. The belief that a lack of love will make your ex-partner want you more.

You have ended the relationship, and at this moment you are not in touch with your former partner. But in the back of your mind, you still harbor the conviction that this is only a temporary arrangement. Surely, they must be suffering from withdrawal in the same way you are. You tell yourself that this situation cannot last, and that they will soon come back to you.

In a mature and stable relationship, distance does indeed make the heart grow fonder. But this is not necessarily the case in a toxic, codependent relationship. When dealing with people with Borderline Personality Disorder, the usual rules do not apply. They might have *object permanence* issues, meaning what is out of sight is out of mind. Moreover, you need to remember just how unstable their feelings are. While being distant may cause your ex-partner to deeply miss you one day, it might also cause them to feel betrayed and resentful on the next.

False Belief #9: The conviction that you must continue to support your former partner.

After the breakup you may still want to stick around your former lover to offer assistance. You may wish to help them obtain care and support them in their daily struggles while maintaining some level of friendship. You need to understand that this attitude is ill-advised and detrimental for both of you. *You are no longer capable of caring for your Borderline ex-partner, no matter how well-intentioned you are.*

There are two main reasons for this. First, the deep feelings still held towards you likely constitute a major destabilizing factor in their life. Surely, you do not mean them any harm. However, due to the history of your relationship, merely seeing you or hearing your voice can cause a whirlwind of emotions and anxiety. Your ex-partner needs to heal and recover without you by their side. The second reason why you cannot be a positive presence for your ex-partner is that you yourself are injured in ways that you may not yet realize. It is essential that you take care of your own wounds before attempting to help others. You have suffered greatly, and you are still suffering. The most important responsibility you have right now is to yourself. If you really care about your former partner and their well-being, it is time to stay away.

False Belief #10: Your trust in their ability to eventually "see the light".

How many times have you thought that your partner has changed – that they have finally understood your point of view and will now turn over a new leaf? How many times have you told yourself that from now on, things will be different? And how many times have you been left bitterly disappointed? The answer is far too many. You have probably gone through several breakups and makeups, in a routine that has become downright poisonous. You must put an end to this toxic vortex and prevent yourself from further perpetuating this unhealthy cycle. Do not be so naïve in thinking that your ex-partner has suddenly transformed or will suddenly transform. You have learned the hard way that things cannot change so easily. You and your former lover were simply playing a game by different sets of rules.

Maintaining No Contact after the Breakup

We have already discussed why under most circumstances you should avoid communication with your Borderline ex-partner. Here are some strategies to help you maintain a no contact policy with them after your breakup. It may be hard to do at first, but you owe it to yourself to move on and begin your healing process.

- Avoid excessive discussion of your ex-partner or your failed relationship with people other than your therapist, at least for the foreseeable future. Always avoid reopening wounds that have not yet had time to fully heal.
- Whenever you feel the urge to get in touch with your former partner, call a friend instead.
- Think about your life before you entered this toxic relationship. Look at old pictures and other objects that may evoke memories of those earlier times.
- Reach out and contact friends that you may have lost touch with after you started the relationship.
- Do not respond to your ex-partner's attempts to get in touch with you. This is important for the mental well-being of you both.
- Be willing to forgive yourself for your mistakes. You may have an occasional slip up. Learn from your errors and promise to be stronger in the future. Allow yourself a degree of leniency but continue to strive for high standards.
- Take up a new hobby such as joining a sports league, a book club, or by doing volunteer work. This not only gives you the opportunity to take your mind off your emotional issues, but it is also a great chance to meet new people.
- Continue to seek psychological support with a therapist. A trained professional will help coach you through these difficult times.

14

Key Points to Remember

It is easy to get caught up in well-intentioned efforts to please and accommodate a partner, regardless of whether they are suffering from a personality disorder. You may find yourself focusing a great deal of energy on them while neglecting your own emotional needs. This is a recipe for anger, sadness, exhaustion, and even physical sickness. *You cannot healthily love someone and sustain a long-term, fulfilling relationship while you yourself are overwhelmed.* You must put your mental well-being first. Learn to listen to your wishes and care for your own needs. All your social interactions will benefit from this attitude, not just your romantic relationships.

Do not shut yourself off from the rest of the world. Make it a point to stay in touch with loved ones who can bring you joy in difficult times. It is important that you are able to occasionally let go and rely on someone else, a person who can listen to you, make you feel cared for, and provide you with reality checks. Build a social network that exists independently from your partner. Set aside time to rest and enjoy yourself.

The following points are valuable regardless of whether you decide to continue or to end the relationship with your Borderline partner.

- **Join a BPD support group.** Meeting other people that are going through, or have gone through, similar experiences will be immensely helpful. This will allow you to experience Borderline Personality Disorder as an external observer, potentially gaining new and valuable insights into your own situation.
- **Keep up with your physical fitness**. Romantic drama can have detrimental effect on one's physical well-being. During such times, you may neglect your heath by eating an excessive amount of junk food, avoiding exercise, or not getting enough sleep. Doing any of these will make you feel worse and will only amplify your problems. If you are healthy and well-rested, you will be better equipped to control your emotions and behavior.
- **Learn to improve communication with your Borderline partner.** Transparently communicating with a Borderline individual can be extremely difficult. Conversing with them can sometimes feel like you are having an argument with a child. They often struggle to understand body language and other types of nonverbal expression. They also may lack a filter to help them determine appropriate topics of conversation. We have already discussed at length how they can say things that are mean, unfair, or irrational. Their fears of abandonment can cause them to overreact to small perceived slights, and their frustration can manifest itself in reckless outbursts and aggression. All these attitudes constitute a huge obstacle to healthy

communication. But by applying the advice discussed in this book, you will be able to make progress. Always try to understand your Borderline partner's emotions. Put yourself in their shoes if you can. This can lead you to compassionate understanding of their condition.

- **Set boundaries in your relationship**. This will establish a clear framework to guide your reactions to unpleasant episodes. It will give an explicit and clear measure for what you can accept in the relationship and what you cannot. Your goal should be to replace the confusion and volatility of the present situation with a sense of order and consistency. *If all parties can learn to respect boundaries, a sense of trust and commitment will be built between you*. Of course, putting boundaries in place is not at all easy in relationships which are characterized by a pattern of instability. When you set new boundaries in your relationship for the first time, your Borderline partner will likely react adversely, and things may initially get worse before improving. But if you give up halfway through, you will just be promoting your loved one's negative behavior and perpetuating the toxic loop in which both of you are stuck. Maintain your commitment and stick to your decisions, as this will fill you with further motivation. In the long run, this attitude can transform your relationship and your life.

15

The Eight-Step Healing Process

This book was written to provide you with concrete, practical advice in dealing with a Borderline partner. Below we summarize the message of the book in eight short steps, whether you decide to stay in the relationship or to leave it.

Read this list to yourself out loud. Then read it again silently and reflect on the meaning of each point. Finally, take out a sheet of paper and write each step in your own handwriting. Carry it with you, or else hang it in a place where you will see it frequently throughout the day.

1. **Recognize** that you have been living in a toxic relationship.
2. **Reflect** on the ways in which you have changed since the beginning of the relationship.
3. **Abandon** false conceptions that prevent you from making progress. Replace them with the positive beliefs expressed in the next three points.
4. **Understand** that you exist independently from your

partner as an individual with a distinct personality with your own needs and desires.

5. **Reinforce** the belief that you deserve to be happy and to satisfy those needs.
6. **Remember** that you alone are ultimately responsible for your own happiness. No one else can take this responsibility from you.
7. **Act** on these three positive beliefs in ways that are conducive to your long-term wellbeing.
8. **Hold** yourself responsible for the choices you make. Once you decide on a course of action, stick to it.

Regardless of whether you choose to continue your relationship or to end it, your life is about to undergo significant changes. Do not be afraid to slip occasionally. No one is perfect. The most important thing is that you prioritize your own mental health. No one deserves to be in a constant state of mental anguish, unsure of the repercussions that might result from upsetting your Borderline partner. You have the ability to regain control of your life. Your story is still being written and you have many positive things waiting for you beyond the horizon. Following the 8-step process outlined above will help you recover.

You owe it to yourself to do this.

Printed in Great Britain
by Amazon

79655843R00071